THE REVIVE CAFE COOKBOOK 7

www.revive.co.nz

Copyright © Revive Concepts Limited 2018
Published by Revive Concepts Limited
First printing 2018 (this book).

ISBN: 978-0-473-45281-0

Also by Jeremy Dixon:
The Revive Cafe Cookbook
The Revive Cafe Cookbook 2
The Revive Cafe Cookbook 3
The Revive Cafe Cookbook 4
The Revive Cafe Cookbook 5
The Revive Cafe Cookbook 6
Cook:30 (Episodes 1-26)
Cook:30.2 (Episodes 27-50)

Produced in New Zealand.
Printed in China.

Recipes: Jeremy Dixon, Kim Stirling
Food Styling & Photography: Jeremy Dixon
Cafe Photography: Elesha Newton, Jeremy Dixon
Graphic Design: Stir Creative, Jeremy Dixon
Recipe testing: Althea Hanna, Annelise Greenfield,
Elisabeth Tupa'i, Evan & Sarinah Ellis, Jeremy Flynn, John
& Esther-Shahn Pedersen, Lynley Stonyer, Sonja Kotze,
Verity Dixon, Vicky Bell, Wayne & Kimberley Hurlow
Proofing: Verity Dixon, Kim Stirling, Dawn McLean,
Virginia Pycroft, John & Esther-Shahn Pedersen,
Nyree Tomkins,

The publisher makes no guarantee as to the availability
of the products in this book. Every effort has been made
to ensure the accuracy of the information presented and
any claims made; however, it is the responsibility of the
reader to ensure the suitability of the product and recipe
for their particular needs. Many natural ingredients vary
in size and texture, and differences in raw ingredients may
marginally affect the outcome of some dishes. Recipes
from the cafes have been adjusted to make them more
appropriate for a home kitchen. All health advice given
in this book is a guideline only. Professional medical or
nutritional advice should be sought for any specific issues.

Metric and imperial measurements have been used in
this cookbook. The tablespoon size used is 15ml (½fl oz),
teaspoon 5ml (⅙fl oz) and cup 250ml (8fl oz). Some
countries use slightly different sized measurements.

Revive Cafes
24 Wyndham St, Auckland Central, New Zealand
33 Lorne St, Auckland Central, New Zealand
P O Box 12-887, Penrose, Auckland 1642, New Zealand
Email: hello@revive.co.nz
Phone: +64-9-303 0420

If you like the recipes in this book I recommend you sign up for weekly inspirational Revive e-mails.
They contain a weekly recipe, cooking and lifestyle tips, the weekly Revive menu, special offers and Revive news.
Visit www.revive.co.nz to sign up or to purchase more copies of this or our other cookbooks online.
Privacy Policy: Revive will never share your details and you can unsubscribe at any time.
facebook.com/cafe.revive   instagram.com/revivecafes

the revive cafe cookbook 7

Delicious & easy plant-powered recipes
from Auckland's popular vegan cafe

WHAT'S ON THE MENU?

104

126

154

SIDES &
FLAVOUR BOOSTERS

VEGAN CHEESES

SWEET TREATS

REVIVE CAFE
UPDATE

Wow! Time flies! It has been 2 years since I created my last cookbook!

This year we have decided to take the big step and become entirely plant-based (or vegan) in the cafes. Virtually all of our food was plant-based anyway, it was just going that final step with a couple of ingredients and dishes.

The hardest part about giving up dairy for most people is giving up cheese. Cheese tastes great and adds awesome flavour and texture.

A special feature of this book is all the wonderful recipes for the plant-based cheeses we have started using at Revive.

There are some commercially available cheeses in most supermarkets, and these are a worthy thing to purchase. However they are usually insanely expensive and often contain very processed starches to stick them together. We have spent many months trialling and researching different cheese recipes. Adjusting and simplifying, adding flavours. The results are awesome. While it is impossible to match dairy based cheese exactly, you will be surprised at how great these vegan cheeses taste. Not to mention their realistic texture.

We have also put a lot of effort into our cafe sweets. In particular, 3 sweets are literally flying out the door as fast as we can make them. In this book I am happy to share our secret recipes! The Pistachio & Rose Cacao Slice (page 164), the Raw Mocca Slice (page 160) and the Tiramisu (page 156) all taste absolutely incredible and you will love how easy they are to make.

You will notice there are a handful of recipes that use millet and is my favourite grain this year. Millet cooks similarly to rice, has a lovely neutral flavour and fluffs up wonderfully for salads and stir fries. Millet is also great under a lovely curry. Make sure you try it!

This year we also invented Nut Butter Frooze Balls as part of our energy balls range. My clever friend and business partner Phil invented a very cool machine to inject peanut butter into our Frooze Balls. This adds a moorish taste and texture experience - everyone loves them. If you haven't already, give them a go!

Vitally Yours!
Jeremy Dixon

COOKBOOK NOTES

GARLIC & GINGER

Garlic and ginger have amazing flavour-enhancing properties and we use both extensively at Revive and in these recipes. Simply chop them up finely before adding to a dish or you can make your own purees by blending the garlic or ginger with a little oil. Alternatively you can purchase pureed ginger from most supermarkets. I do not recommend buying pureed garlic as I find it has an unpleasant odour and flavour.

OILS

Where an unspecified "oil" is mentioned you can use your preferred oil. I generally use coconut, rice bran or grape seed for cooking applications, such as sauteing onions, and virgin olive oil for cold applications like dressings.

SWEETENERS

I use a range of low-refined sweeteners in my recipes. These include maple syrup, date puree, honey and coconut sugar. You can often interchange and use your favourite sweetener in most recipes. Other healthy sweeteners include apple sauce and agave. To make up a batch of date puree (which is my favourite excellent and inexpensive sweetener), simply blend equal parts of dried dates and water until it is a smooth puree.

NUTS

Nuts are used in many dishes at Revive and in this cookbook. Unless specified, raw nuts are used. Having the wrong sort of nut will not affect the outcome of most recipes as they are often interchangeable. You can use nut pieces if you want to minimise cost. Roasted nuts are usually used where they are presented whole (in salads or stir fries) so they maintain their crunchiness and do not go soggy.

CREAMS

Different methods are used to make some dishes creamy. Coconut cream, almond cream and cashew cream can usually be used interchangeably in hotpots and soups.

TOFU

I generally use a firm tofu. Most savoury recipes can handle a firmer or softer tofu by simply adjusting the cooking time. However there are times when the type of tofu used can have an impact on a dish, some sweets dishes in particular may come out differently.

BEANS/CHICKPEAS

I have specified canned beans/chickpeas (garbanzo beans) in the recipes as this is the most convenient. Drain before using.
If you can use freshly cooked beans they will taste better and are significantly cheaper. One can of beans is around 2 cups.
I recommend you soak and cook your own beans and store them in the freezer. You will need to soak them overnight in plenty of water (they expand approximately three times their volume). Drain and rinse the soaked beans then cook in fresh water until soft, which will be between 30 minutes and 2 hours, depending on the bean and its age. Once they are cooked, drain and leave to cool. Transfer to small containers for easy use and freeze. To defrost, simply run some hot water over them in a sieve or colander for 30 seconds.

COOKING GRAINS

I recommend that you cook extra grains like rice and quinoa and store in your refrigerator for an easy ingredient to use in the following few days. When you cook grains remember to use boiling water to save time, and first bring the grain to the boil before turning down to a simmer. Do not stir while cooking and keep the lid on. Cooking times are provided in the recipe methods.

COOKING TERMS

Saute: to cook food on a high heat and in a little oil while stirring with a wooden spoon.
Simmer: to have food cooking at a low heat setting so it is just bubbling.
Roast: to bake in the oven coated with a little oil. Use the fan bake setting to achieve more even cooking.

MIXING

You can mix most recipes in the pot you are cooking in or in a large mixing bowl. When mixing, stir gently so as not to damage the food. With salads, mix with your hands if possible. Gently lift up the salad ingredients and let them fall down naturally with gravity.

TASTE TEST

It is difficult to get a recipe that works 100% the same every time, especially when you are using natural and fresh ingredients. Sizes in vegetables vary, spices and herbs differ in strength of flavour and you can even get differences in evaporation rates with different sized pots. Make sure you taste test every dish before you serve and be willing to add a little more cooking time or more seasoning if necessary.

PROCESSORS & BLENDERS

Some recipes require a food processor (usually with an S blade). Other recipes require a blender or liquidiser (usually a tall jug with 4 pronged blades) or a stick blender (immersion blender).

QUANTITIES

The quantities for each dish are an estimate and will vary depending on cooking times and ingredient size. I have used one cup as an average serving size.

GLUTEN FREE & DAIRY FREE

A large proportion of the recipes are gluten free and all are dairy free. If you have any allergies you will need to check that each recipe is suitable.

8 KEYS TO
HEALTHY LIVING

Water: drink at least 2 litres (2 quarts) of pure water per day.

Water

THESE ARE THE HEALTH PRINCIPLES THAT REVIVE IS FOUNDED ON. TO HAVE COMPLETE ENERGY AND VITALITY, IT IS NOT ENOUGH TO JUST EAT HEALTHY FOOD. THERE ARE OTHER SIMPLE THINGS THAT CREATE GOOD HEALTH, SUMMARISED BY THESE 8 KEYS.

THE GOOD NEWS IS THAT IF YOU APPLY THESE 8 SIMPLE STEPS IN YOUR DAY-TO-DAY LIVING YOU WILL HAVE TREMENDOUSLY MORE ENERGY AND VITALITY, AVOID DISEASE AND MOST LIKELY ADD ANOTHER 20 YEARS TO YOUR LIFE!!!

Temperance: free yourself from stimulants like alcohol, energy drinks, coffee and drugs.

Temperance

Nutrition: eat plant-based foods, fresh produce and avoid processed foods and sugars.

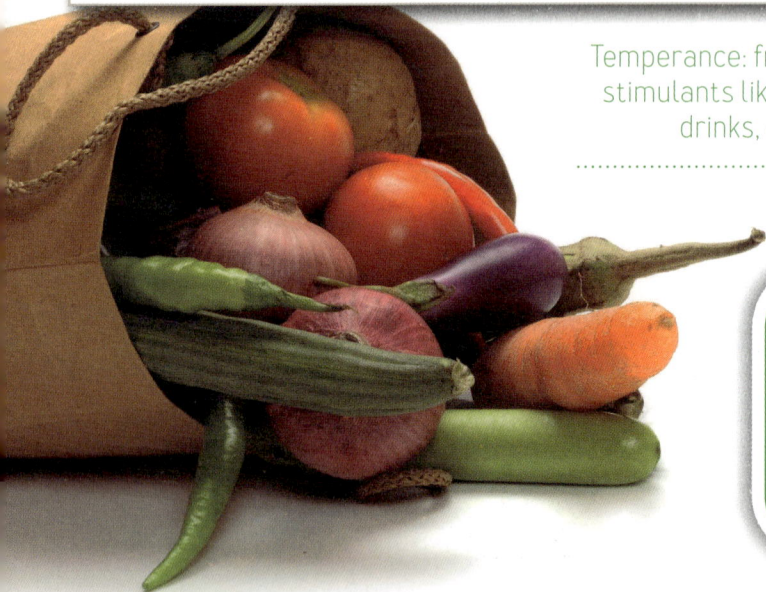

Nutrition

Sunshine: aim for 10 minutes minimum per day.

Sunshine

Trust

Trust: live at peace with everyone and your God.

Rest: get 8 hours quality sleep every night.

Rest

Air

Air: breathe deeply - start every day with 10 deep breaths.

Exercise: get at least 30 minutes every day.

Exercise

SALADS

HOTPOTS, SOUPS & STIR FRIES

MAIN MEALS

SIDES &
FLAVOUR
BOOSTERS

VEGAN
CHEESES

SWEET
TREATS

SALADS

CRISPY & JUICY
THAI TOFU PEANUT
SALAD WITH LIME & PEANUT DRESSING

I love Thai flavours and this salad tastes amazing. It is so crunchy and the fresh coriander and mint make it extra special. This salad can be a main meal or a side dish.

MAKES 7 X 1 CUP SERVES

600g (18oz) tofu cut into large cubes

1 tablespoon oil

½ teaspoon salt

1 cup carrot julienned

½ cup red capsicum (bell pepper) finely sliced

½ cup yellow capsicum (bell pepper) finely sliced

1 cup red cabbage finely sliced

1 cup savoy (wrinkly) cabbage finely sliced

¼ cup fresh coriander (cilantro) finely chopped

¼ cup mint finely sliced

½ cup roasted peanuts

LIME & PEANUT DRESSING

1 tablespoon Thai red curry paste

½ cup water

4 tablespoons peanut butter

2 tablespoons lime juice (around 2 limes)

1 tablespoon honey or date puree

1 Place the cubed tofu and oil in a non-stick pan and saute, stirring regularly, for 10 minutes or until the tofu is golden brown. Sprinkle salt over.

2 Combine the vegetables, herbs, peanuts and sauteed tofu in a salad dish and gently mix.

3 Add all the dressing ingredients to a blender and blend until smooth.

4 Drizzle half the dressing over the top so you do not drown the salad. Put the remaining dressing on the edge or in a separate bowl.

FRESH BASIL
CAPRESE SALAD
WITH PLANT-POWERED MOZZARELLA

Basil, tomato and plant-powered mozzarella combine together to make an awesomely tasty salad.

MAKES 4 X 1 CUP SERVES

3 cups mozzarella balls (page 136) sliced in half

3 cups small tomatoes (mixed colours) quartered

1 cup cherry tomatoes (mixed colours) halved

2 tablespoons olive oil

garnish: ½ cup fresh basil roughly chopped

garnish: ¼ teaspoon flaky sea salt

1   Lay plant-powered mozzarella and tomatoes on a platter.

2   Drizzle olive oil over the top. Sprinkle with salt and scatter over basil.

MINTY & CRUNCHY
VERY GREEN SALAD
WITH MAPLE TAHINI DRESSING

I needed a fresh salad for a potluck and this is one of those "use up everything in the fridge" recipes. If not serving immediately, assemble all the ingredients and toss just before serving.

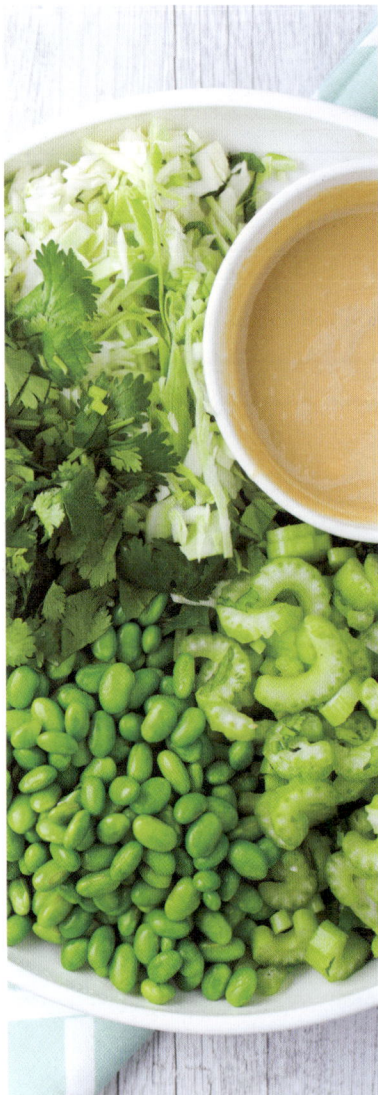

MAKES 8 X 1 CUP SERVES

3 cups cabbage finely sliced

3 cups celery finely sliced

1 cup mint finely sliced

½ cup coriander (cilantro) finely sliced

2 cups edamame (green soy beans) (usually purchased frozen)

MAPLE TAHINI DRESSING

3 tablespoons tahini (sesame seed paste)

3 tablespoons lemon juice

1 teaspoon ginger puree or ginger finely chopped

3 tablespoons maple syrup

½ teaspoon salt

1 Arrange vegetables, herbs and edamame on a large platter.

2 Mix the dressing ingredients in a bowl until smooth.

TIP You may need to adjust the consistency by adding more tahini or water to create a creamy and easily pourable dressing.

3 Before serving, mix vegetables and herbs together and drizzle the dressing over the top.

ENTICING
SPRING BITTER GREENS
SALAD

This is a fresh salad with a base of bitter greens combined with some amazing colours, textures and flavours. I think it is great without a dressing.

MAKES 8 X 1 CUP SERVES

2 cups lettuce mix containing bitter greens

200g (6oz) cherry tomatoes (mixed colours) cut in half

1 avocado cubed

½ cup red cabbage finely sliced

1 cup yellow courgette (zucchini) sliced and quartered (around 1 courgette)

4 radishes finely sliced

1 red capsicum (bell pepper) finely sliced

1 Spray the greens with cold water to liven them up.

2 In a mixing bowl add all ingredients and mix gently.

3 Lift out carefully with your hands and place on a serving platter.

TIP If you must have a dressing, simply drizzle over a little lemon juice and olive oil.

CHICKPEA
PANEER & ROOT VEGE
SALAD WITH WALNUTS

This amazingly tasty salad takes a little extra time to wait while roasting vegetables, but it is worth it!

MAKES 6 X 1 CUP SERVES

2 cups beetroot cut into small wedges (around 2 beetroot)

2 cups carrots cut into small wedges (around 1 large carrot)

2 teaspoons oil

¼ teaspoon salt

3 cups cos or iceberg lettuce sliced/ripped

2 cups chickpea paneer (page 138)

¼ cup walnuts roughly chopped

¼ cup pumpkin seeds

garnish: mint leaves

dressing: ¼ cup lime & cashew aioli (page 122)

1 Put beetroot in a bowl 1 teaspoon of oil and ⅛ teaspoon of salt.

2 Mix it all around until evenly coated and place on a baking tray with baking (parchment) paper.

3 Repeat with carrots. Do not mingle with the beetroot to avoid red colour transfer.

4 Bake at 180°C (350°F) for 45 minutes or until soft.

5 Layer up the ingredients on a platter. Start with lettuce, roasted vegetables and paneer and then add remaining ingredients.

6 Garnish with mint leaves and drizzle aioli over the top.

RED QUINOA MINGLE
WITH EGGPLANT & COURGETTES

MAKES 4 X 1 CUP SERVES

....

½ cup red quinoa

1 cup boiling water

1 tablespoon oil

2 cloves garlic crushed or
finely chopped

1 cup onion finely diced (around
1 onion)

½ cup coriander (cilantro) stalks
finely sliced (reserve leaves
for garnish)

1 cup courgette (zucchini) diced
5mm (¼in)

2 cups eggplant (aubergine) diced
5mm (¼in)

½ teaspoon salt

½ cup kalamata olives (pitted)

garnish: ¼ cup red onion (around ¼
onion) finely diced

garnish: fresh coriander (cilantro)
roughly chopped

When summer vegetables are
available, I love buying eggplants and
courgettes and adding them to many
dishes. This recipe can be a meal in
its own right, chilled as a salad, or
presented as a side dish.

....

1 Put the quinoa and water into a pot
and bring to the boil. Put the lid on,
turn down the heat and simmer for 12
minutes or until the quinoa has cooked.
Leave to sit for 10 minutes and then fluff
up with a fork.

2 In a pot or pan saute the oil, garlic,
onion, coriander stalks, courgette and
eggplant for 8 minutes or until soft.

3 Add the cooked quinoa, salt and olives.

4 Transfer to your serving dish and
garnish with red onion and
fresh coriander.

REFRESHING LIME
ASIAN MISO QUINOA
SALAD WITH MISO DRESSING

A fusion of South American quinoa with delicate Asian flavours make this an excellent salad that can also double as a light lunch.

MAKES 6 X 1 CUP SERVES

1½ cups cooked quinoa (½ cup raw quinoa and 1 cup boiling water)

1 cup red onion (around 1 red onion) finely sliced

1 tablespoon ginger puree or ginger finely chopped

2 cloves garlic crushed or finely chopped

1 tablespoon oil

1 cup red capsicum (bell pepper) finely chopped (around 1 capsicum)

1 cup red cabbage finely sliced

1 cup edamame (green soy beans) frozen

1 cup carrots julienne (around 1 carrot)

2 tablespoons black sesame seeds

2 tablespoons white sesame seeds

1 teaspoon salt

garnish: fresh coriander (cilantro)

garnish: lime wedges

MISO DRESSING

½ to 1 tablespoon miso paste

2 tablespoons tahini (sesame seed paste)

2 tablespoons honey or date puree

2 tablespoons lemon juice

2 tablespoon olive oil

1 tablespoon white sesame seeds

1 tablespoon ginger puree or ginger finely chopped

½ teaspoon salt

2 tablespoons water

1 Put quinoa and water in a pot. Place the lid on and bring to boil. Turn down to a simmer (just bubbling) and cook for 12 minutes or until the water has disappeared. Leave to sit for 10 minutes and then fluff up with a fork.

2 In a small bowl combine all of the dressing ingredients and stir.

TIP Some miso pastes are very strong so start with half the amount and taste, and then add more if necessary.

3 In a pot or pan saute the onion, ginger, garlic and oil for 5 minutes or until soft.

4 Add the cooked quinoa and all other ingredients (except dressing) and stir well.

5 Transfer to a platter and pour over the dressing.

6 Garnish with coriander and lime wedges.

TIP This salad can be served warm or chilled.

RAINBOW
CHICKPEA MINGLE
WITH KALE & POMEGRANATE

This is a great colourful salad. The key is to cook the kale and cabbage just slightly so it is not totally raw, but is not fully cooked.

MAKES 6 X 1 CUP SERVES

2 cloves garlic crushed or finely chopped

1 teaspoon oil

3 cups kale finely sliced

2 cups red cabbage finely sliced

¼ teaspoon salt

400g (12oz) can chickpeas (garbanzo beans) drained (around 1½ cups)

½ cup pomegranate seeds

dressing: ¼ cup lime & cashew aioli (page 122)

garnish: 1 tablespoon sesame seeds

1 In a pot or pan cook the garlic and oil for 1 minute or until the garlic is soft. Take care as garlic burns easily.

2 Immediately add in the kale, cabbage and salt and toss around for 2 minutes or until slightly soft and warmed. Sprinkle with salt.

3 Transfer to a platter and spread out. Top with the chickpeas and pomegranate seeds.

4 Drizzle over aioli and garnish with sesame seeds.

TIP Make sure you do not overcook the kale and cabbage, if in doubt it is better undercooked.

SUMMER
COURGETTE & MILLET
SALAD

Millet is a great alternative to quinoa or rice. It has a very neutral flavour and is light and fluffy. Add a little love with some Mediterranean ingredients and you can create a delicious salad like this one. Serve warm or chilled.

MAKES 5 X 1 CUP SERVES

1½ cups cooked millet (½ cup raw hulled millet and 1 cup boiling water)

2 cups courgettes (zucchini) halved and cut into half moons (around 2 courgettes)

1 tablespoon oil

1 clove garlic crushed or finely chopped

¼ cup red onion (around ¼ red onion) roughly diced

½ teaspoon salt

½ teaspoon turmeric

¼ cup pumpkin seeds

1 cup kalamata olives (pitted)

¼ cup fresh mint finely sliced

garnish: extra mint

garnish: 1 tablespoon lemon juice (around ½ lemon)

1   Put millet and water in a pot. Place the lid on and bring to boil. Turn down to a simmer (just bubbling) and cook for 20 minutes or until the water has disappeared. Leave to sit for 10 minutes and then fluff up with a fork.

2   In a pan saute the courgettes, oil, garlic and red onion for 7 minutes or until everything is soft.

3   Add the millet to the pan with courgettes and stir in with salt and turmeric and cook for another 2 minutes.

4   Stir in remaining ingredients and serve.

5   Garnish with extra mint and lemon juice.

TIP   Make sure you use hulled millet. Unhulled millet is tough and usually sold as bird seed.

THAI
TOFU PEANUT MINGLE
WITH CAULIFLOWER & THAI AIOLI

The Revive salad bar usually contains a "mingle" salad. Each week we change it around and see if we can come up with a new amazing combination. I've noticed that mingles like this one, with tofu and some kind of Thai flavours, are always popular!

MAKES 6 X 1 CUP SERVES

300g (10oz) firm tofu (around 1 block) cut into 1cm (½in) cubes

1 tablespoon oil

2 cups cauliflower florets (around ¼ small cauliflower)

4 cups boiling water

2 cups spinach roughly chopped

¼ cup red onion (around ¼ red onion) finely sliced

½ cup chopped roasted peanuts

2 tablespoons lemon grass (frozen)

1 tablespoon ginger puree or ginger finely chopped

½ cup red capsicum (bell pepper) finely chopped (around ½ capsicum)

1 teaspoon salt

garnish: chopped roasted peanuts

THAI AIOLI

¾ cup cashew nuts

½ clove garlic crushed or finely chopped

2 tablespoons lime juice (around 2 limes)

3 tablespoons water

2 teaspoons maple syrup

⅛ teaspoon salt

1 tablespoon Thai red curry paste

1 In a pot or pan saute the tofu and oil for 10 minutes or until the tofu has browned and the water has evaporated, giving it a chewy texture.

2 Put the cauliflower into a pot with boiling water and cook for 4 minutes or until tender. Drain immediately to prevent further cooking.

3 In a bowl combine the tofu, cauliflower and all other non-dressing ingredients and mix gently.

4 Put the aioli ingredients into a blender and blend until smooth.

5 Place salad on a platter and drizzle with the aioli. Garnish with extra peanuts.

BUTTERNUT, BLACK BEAN &
BARLEY SALAD
WITH GREEN DRESSING

This is a lovely chewy, fresh and nutritious salad. The addition of raw pumpkin gives it a lovely earthy flavour.

MAKES 8 X 1 CUP SERVES

2 cups cooked pearl barley (¾ cup raw pearl barley and 1½ cups boiling water)

400g (12oz) can black beans drained (around 1½ cups)

2 cups raw butternut pumpkin peeled, finely julienned or grated

1 cup green capsicum diced (around 1 capsicum)

2 cups sweet corn (frozen, canned, or fresh)

2 tablespoons parsley finely chopped

¼ cup sun-dried tomatoes sliced

garnish: fresh coriander (cilantro)

GREEN DRESSING

2 tablespoons lime juice (around 2 limes)

2 teaspoons cider vinegar

1 tablespoon olive oil

½ cup fresh coriander (cilantro)

2 tablespoons honey or date puree

1 teaspoon salt

2 teaspoons dijon mustard

1 Put pearl barley and water in a pot. Heat until bubbling and turn down to a simmer with the lid on. Cook for 30-40 minutes or until soft and water has been absorbed.

2 Put dressing ingredients into a blender and blend until smooth.

3 Combine cooked barley and other ingredients in a bowl and mix gently.

4 Stir in dressing and serve with a garnish of fresh coriander.

FUNKY WARM
ROAST CAULIFLOWER
SALAD

A lovely warming winter salad with strong Mediterranean flavours.

MAKES 5 X 1 CUP SERVES

6 cups cauliflower cut into small florets (1 medium cauliflower)

2 teaspoons oil

2 cups courgettes (zucchini) cut into ½cm (¼in) slices (around 2 courgettes)

1 teaspoon oil

½ teaspoon salt

¼ cup kalamata olives (pitted)

¼ cup cashew nuts roasted

¼ cup sun-dried tomatoes roughly sliced

¼ cup fresh coriander (cilantro) chopped

1 On an oven tray lined with baking (parchment) paper mix the cauliflower and 2 teaspoons of oil. Bake at 180°C (350°F) for 30 minutes or until soft.

2 In a pot or pan saute the courgettes and 1 teaspoon of oil for 4 minutes or until just soft and slightly golden.

3 Combine all ingredients in a bowl and gently mix.

TIP This salad can be served warm or chilled.

DELECTABLE
HERBED BABY POTATO
SALAD WITH HONEY MUSTARD DRESSING

The celery and celery seeds give this salad a lovely crunch and zingy flavour.
Serve warm or chilled.

MAKES 8 X 1 CUP SERVES

8 cups baby potatoes halved
(around 20 baby potatoes or
around 1kg (2lb))

1 tablespoon oil

2 cups celery sliced thinly
(around 2 large stalks)

½ cup Italian parsley
finely chopped

1 tablespoon celery seeds

½ cup red onion (around ½ red
onion) thinly sliced

½ teaspoon salt

garnish: chopped parsley

HONEY MUSTARD DRESSING

3 tablespoons olive oil

2 teaspoons seeded
(wholegrain) mustard

1 tablespoon almond milk or
other plant-based milk

2 teaspoons honey or date puree

1 tablespoon lemon juice

¼ teaspoon salt

1 clove garlic crushed or
finely chopped

1 In a bowl coat the potatoes with oil. Pour
out onto a baking tray lined with baking
(parchment) paper.

2 Bake at 180°C (350°F) for 30 minutes or
until soft.

3 Combine dressing ingredients in a small bowl
and mix until smooth.

4 Combine cooked potatoes, dressing and
other ingredients and mix gently.

5 Serve with a garnish of parsley.

ASIAN AVOCADO &
MISO TOFU STRIP
SALAD

Chicken salads are popular in "normal" restaurants. This is my healthy vegetarian alternative. The miso gives the tofu a lovely flavour!

MAKES 6 X 1 CUP SERVES

600g (20oz) firm tofu cut into 1cm (½in) slabs

1 tablespoon oil

½ teaspoon salt

1 to 3 tablespoons miso paste

4 tablespoons lemon juice (around 2 lemons)

1 red capsicum finely sliced

1 avocado cut into cubes

1 cup celery cut into cubes (around 1 large stalk)

¼ cup red onion (around ¼ red onion) finely sliced

garnish: 1 tablespoon maple syrup

garnish: 1 tablespoon sesame seeds

1 In a non-stick pan saute the tofu, oil and salt for 10 minutes or until firm.

2 Spoon 1 tablespoon of the miso paste onto the tofu and stir around.

TIP Depending on the strength of your miso you may need to add more. If your miso is very thick you may need to mix it with a little water first .

3 Continue to cook for a further 10 minutes or until the tofu becomes slightly charred.

4 Put the tofu onto a chopping board and slice into strips.

5 Toss all the ingredients together, garnish with sesame seeds and serve warm.

6 Garnish with a drizzle of maple syrup and some sesame seeds. Serve warm.

HOTPOTS, SOUPS & STIR FRIES

SMOKY
PINTO BEAN & YAM
CASSEROLE

MAKES 8 X 1 CUP SERVES

....

4 cups yams (oca) (around 16 yams)

1 tablespoon oil

2 cloves garlic crushed or finely chopped

1 cup onion finely diced (around 1 onion)

1 tablespoon oil

2 teaspoons cumin powder

2 teaspoons smoked paprika

½ cup water

2 teaspoons salt

4 cups button mushrooms halved

400g (12oz) can crushed tomatoes

1 tablespoon tomato paste

2 x 400g (12oz) cans pinto beans (around 3 cups)

garnish: red onion diced

garnish: chilli finely sliced

garnish: coriander (cilantro)

This is a lovely thick, warming hotpot with the added bonus of some delicious roasted yams (oca). Serve over rice, pasta or quinoa.

....

1 Place the yams on an oven tray. Drizzle oil on top and shake around so they are evenly coated. Bake at 180°C (350°F) for 40 minutes or until soft.

2 In a pot or pan saute the garlic, onion and oil for 5 minutes or until soft.

3 Add the cumin and smoked paprika and stir for 30 seconds.

4 Add the water, salt and mushrooms and cook for 10 minutes or until the water has disappeared and the mushrooms are soft.

5 Add the tomatoes and tomato paste and stir well. Add the beans and continue to heat, stirring gently, until just bubbling.

6 Put the roasted yams on top and garnish with red onion, chillies and coriander.

TIP Instead of pinto beans you can use any other white bean such as butter (lima) beans or cannellini beans.

THAI
VERY GREEN DAHL
WITH REVIVE CUCUMBER RAITA

MAKES 6 X 1 CUP SERVES

....

1 cup onion finely diced
(around 1 onion)

2 cloves garlic crushed or
finely chopped

1 tablespoon ginger puree
or ginger finely chopped

1 tablespoon oil

1 cup red lentils

2½ cups boiling water

1 tablespoon honey or
date puree

½ teaspoon salt

1 tablespoon Thai green
curry paste

1 cup courgette (zucchini)
grated (around 1 courgette)

1 cup kale finely sliced
(around 2 leaves without
the thick stalk)

1 cup frozen peas

½ cup fresh coriander
(cilantro) finely sliced

serve with: Revive
cucumber raita (page 120)

I love dahl! So simple and warming. This one
has a lot of "green stuff" with amazing flavours.
Serve on rice, millet or quinoa. For extra creamy
deliciousness add some Revive cucumber raita!

....

1 In a pot or pan saute the onion, garlic, ginger and oil
for 5 minutes or until soft.

2 Add the lentils and water and simmer (just
bubbling) with lid off for 20 minutes or until the
water has disappeared. Stir regularly.

3 Stir in the honey, salt and curry paste. If your curry
paste is thick mix it with a little water first so it
mixes in easily.

4 Add the green vegetables and fresh coiander and
cook for around 2 minutes to just heat them up and
soften them.

TIP Do not overcook the greens or they will
lose their flavour, texture and vibrant
green colour.

5 Serve immediately with a dollop of raita
on top.

TIP Instead of kale you can use spinach or
silverbeet (swiss chard).

SPICY
TANDOORI QUINOA
WITH ROAST PARSNIP & CHICKPEAS

This is a lovely hotpot with grains in it, a hum of heat and soft, flavoursome parsnips for something a little different.

MAKES 6 X 1 CUP SERVES

1½ cups cooked quinoa (½ cup raw quinoa and 1 cup boiling water)

1½ cups parsnip finely diced (around 2 parsnips)

1 teaspoon oil

1 cup onion finely diced (around 1 onion)

2 cloves garlic crushed or finely chopped

1 tablespoon ginger puree or ginger finely chopped

1 tablespoon oil

¼ teaspoon cayenne pepper

1 tablespoon garam masala

1 tablespoon sweet paprika

400g (12oz) can crushed tomatoes

400g (12oz) can chickpeas (garbanzo beans) drained (around 1½ cups)

1 cup hot water

2 tablespoons honey or date puree

1 teaspoon salt

2 tablespoons lime juice (around 2 limes)

garnish: fresh coriander (cilantro) chopped

garnish: red onion finely diced

garnish: vegan yoghurt (optional)

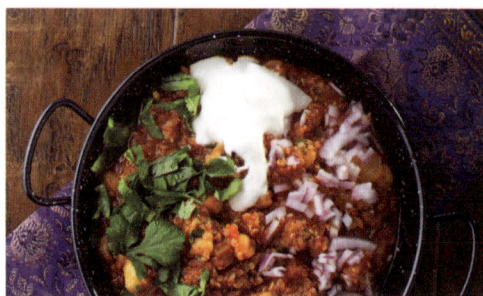

1 Put quinoa and water in a pot. Place the lid on and bring to boil. Turn down to a simmer (just bubbling) and cook for 12 minutes or until the water has disappeared. Leave to sit for 10 minutes and then fluff up with a fork.

2 Put parsnip in a bowl with the oil. Mix around until evenly coated and put on a baking tray with baking (parchment) paper. Bake at 180°C (350°F) for 15 minutes or until soft.

3 In a pot or pan saute the onion, garlic, ginger and oil for 5 minutes or until soft.

4 Add the spices and stir for 30 seconds to activate the flavour.

5 Stir in the cooked quinoa, cooked parsnip and remaining ingredients and heat until it is just bubbling.

6 Serve garnished with fresh coriander, red onion and a vegan yoghurt.

INDIAN
SAAG PANEER

This is a popular Indian takeaway dish. However it is usually very heavy on cream and cheese. This version replaces the paneer cheese with a chickpea version, and uses coconut cream to make it creamy!

MAKES 6 X 1 CUP SERVES

1 cup onion finely diced (around 1 onion)

2 cloves garlic crushed or finely chopped

1 tablespoon oil

1 tablespoon garam masala

1 teaspoon salt

¼ cup hot water

500g (16oz) bag frozen spinach

1 cup coconut cream

2 cups chickpea paneer (page 138)

garnish: fresh coriander (cilantro)

1 In a pot or pan saute the onions, garlic and oil for 5 minutes or until soft.

2 Stir in garam masala for 30 seconds to activate the flavour in the spice.

3 Add the salt, water and spinach. Cook for 5 minutes or until the spinach has defrosted. Stir in the coconut cream.

4 Put three quarters of the mixture into a blender and blend until smooth. Pour this back into the pan with the unblended mixture.

5 Add the chickpea paneer and heat until it is nearly boiling (but do not let bubble).

6 Serve with a garnish of fresh coriander.

TIP You could use cubed firm tofu as an alternative to the chickpea paneer.

MUSHROOM POTATO &
TEMPEH SATAY

This was created by a "what's in the fridge" moment and surpassed my expectations. You do not always have to specially make a satay sauce. You can cheat like in this recipe and just add some peanut butter and Thai curry paste.

MAKES 5 X 1 CUP SERVES

2 cups baby potatoes quartered

4 cups button mushrooms halved

1 cup onion finely diced (around 1 onion)

2 cloves garlic crushed or finely chopped

2 tablespoons ginger puree or ginger finely chopped

1 tablespoon oil

400g (12oz) can crushed tomatoes

1 teaspoon salt

1 tablespoon honey or date puree

¾ cup peanut butter

1 tablespoon Thai red curry paste

1 cup hot water

250g (8oz) block of tempeh (fermented soy beans) cubed

1 tablespoon oil

2 cups spinach finely sliced

½ cup snow peas

garnish: ½ cup capsicum (bell pepper) finely sliced

garnish: ¼ cup fresh coriander (cilantro) finely sliced

optional garnish: chopped roasted peanuts

1 In a pot cook the potatoes in boiling water for 15 minutes or until soft. Drain.

2 In a pot or pan saute the mushrooms, onion, garlic, ginger and oil for 5 minutes or until soft.

3 Add the tomatoes, salt and honey.

4 In a small bowl mix the peanut butter, curry paste and water together to form a paste. Add to the satay.

5 In a separate pot or pan saute the tempeh and oil for 7 minutes or until golden brown. Add to the cooked satay.

6 Add the cooked potatoes, spinach and snow peas and stir through briefly.

7 Garnish with capsicum and fresh coriander. Optionally garnish with roasted peanuts.

TIP Instead of tempeh you can use other protein sources such as tofu, chickpeas or other beans.

THICK & CHUNKY WINTER WARMING
CAULIFLOWER SOUP

This is a great soup for a cold winter's day. The cashew cream and stock powder transform this vegetable from ordinary to awesome!

MAKES 10 X 1 CUP SERVES

2 cups red onion finely diced

2 cloves garlic crushed or finely chopped

5 cups cauliflower very finely chopped (around 1 medium head)

1 cup carrot finely chopped (around 1 carrot)

1 tablespoon oil

4 cups boiling water

1 cup cashews

3 tablespoons Revive stock powder (page 123)

1 cup cold water

1½ teaspoons salt

4 tablespoons lemon juice (around 2 lemons)

garnish: fresh coriander (cilantro) chopped

1 In a pot saute the onion, garlic, cauliflower, carrots and oil for 10 minutes.

2 Add boiling water and cook for a further 10 minutes or until cauliflower is soft.

3 Put the cashews, stock powder and cold water in a blender and blend until silky smooth.

4 To the blender add 2 cups of the cooked vegetable mix. Blend and then add back into the main pot.

5 Add salt and lemon juice and stir in.

6 Serve with a garnish of fresh coriander.

TIP If you want a smooth soup just blend all of the vegetable mix.

BUTTER BEAN &
BROCCOLI SOUP

This is a really simple soup but very delicious. You will not know there are beans in this soup but they give it a really silky texture.

MAKES 6 X 1 CUP SERVES

1 cup onion roughly diced (around 1 onion)

2 cloves garlic crushed or finely chopped

2 cups celery sliced (around 1 large stalk)

1 tablespoon oil

4 cups broccoli roughly chopped (around 1 large head)

400g (12oz) can butter (lima) beans (around 1½ cups)

4 cups boiling water

1 teaspoon salt

1 cup cashew cream (½ cup cashew nuts and 1 cup hot water)

garnish: parsley finely chopped

1 In a pot saute the onion, garlic, celery and oil for 5 minutes or until soft.

2 Add the broccoli, beans, water and salt and cook for 5 minutes or until the broccoli is tender. Do not over cook.

3 Blend with a stick blender until smooth. Alternatively tip into a blender, blend, and pour back into the pot.

4 Make the cashew cream by putting the cashews and hot water in a blender to soak for 10 minutes. Then blend until very smooth. Pour most of the cream into the soup and mix. Reserve a little for a garnish.

5 Serve garnished with a drizzle of cashew cream and a sprinkle of parsley.

TIP To make the garnish cream look interesting you can use the end of a fork to roughen it up.

CREAMY & COCONUTTY
THAI LIME BISQUE
WITH SHITAKE MUSHROOMS

This has a lovely mixture of flavoursome Thai ingredients.

MAKES 5 X 1 CUP SERVES

40g dry shitake mushrooms
(makes around 1 cup soaked)

3 cups boiling water

1 cup onion finely diced (around
1 onion)

2 cloves garlic crushed or
finely chopped

1 tablespoon ginger puree or
ginger finely chopped

2 tablespoons lemongrass finely
chopped (fresh, from a jar
or frozen)

1 teaspoon oil

1 tablespoon Thai red curry paste

1 teaspoon sesame oil

1 teaspoon salt

¼ cup lime juice (around 4 limes)

1 cup coconut cream

garnish: spring onions
finely sliced

garnish: fresh coriander (cilantro)
finely sliced

garnish: coconut cream

1 Put the mushrooms in a bowl and cover with the boiling water. Let sit for 5 minutes to soften. Do not drain.

2 In a pot or pan saute the onion, garlic, ginger, lemongrass and oil for 5 minutes or until soft. Add the mushrooms and soaking water and cook for a further 3 minutes.

3 Add the curry paste, sesame oil, salt and lime juice.

4 Blend with a stick blender until smooth. Alternatively tip into a blender, blend, and pour back into the pot.

5 Continue to heat until boiling. Turn the heat off and stir in the coconut cream.

6 Serve with a garnish of spring onions, fresh coriander (cilantro) and a drizzle of coconut cream.

TIP Shitake mushrooms are found in Asian stores and some supermarkets.

CHUNKY MUSHROOM & BEAN SOUP

Thick, creamy, hearty, mushroomy. A substantial soup for winter that you will love. It is actually so thick it could double as a hotpot.

MAKES 7 X 1 CUP SERVES

1 cup onion finely diced (around 1 onion)

2 cloves garlic crushed or finely chopped

1 teaspoon dried thyme

4 cups button mushrooms finely sliced

1 tablespoon ginger puree or ginger finely chopped

1 cup celery finely diced (around 1 large stalk)

1 tablespoon oil

400g (12oz) can crushed tomatoes

2 tablespoons tomato paste

1 tablespoon honey or date puree

1 teaspoon salt

1 cup water

1 cup cashew cream (½ cup cashew nuts and 1 cup hot water)

2 x 400g (12oz) cans butter (lima) beans drained (around 3 cups)

garnish: parsley finely chopped

1 In a pot or pan saute the onions, garlic, thyme, mushrooms, ginger, celery and oil for 7 minutes or until onion is soft and mushrooms have halved in size.

2 Add tomatoes, tomato paste, honey, salt and water and heat until it just starts to bubble.

3 Make the cashew cream by putting the cashews and hot water in a blender to soak for 5 minutes. Then blend until very smooth. Pour into the soup.

4 Stir in the butter beans. Heat for a further 3 minutes or until well heated.

5 Serve with a garnish of parsley.

TIP If you cannot find butter (lima) beans you can use any other white bean.

TANGY
MILLET & LENTIL HASH
WITH SWEET POTATO

You may be thinking baby food with these ingredients, but think again. Lovely flavours and a creamy texture make this an awesome meal or side dish.

MAKES 5 X 1 CUP SERVES

1½ cups cooked millet (½ cup raw hulled millet and 1 cup boiling water)

1 cup onion finely diced (around 1 onion)

1 tablespoon oil

1 tablespoon ginger puree or ginger finely chopped

2 cloves garlic crushed or finely sliced

2 cups orange kumara (sweet potato) grated (around 1 medium kumara)

1 cup celery finely diced (around 1 large stalk)

400g (12oz) can brown lentils drained (around 1½ cups)

1 cup frozen peas

1 teaspoon salt

garnish: 2 tablespoons lemon juice (around 1 lemon)

garnish: 2 tablespoons red onion finely diced

garnish: ½ cup fresh coriander (cilantro) finely sliced

1 Put millet and water in a pot. Place the lid on and bring to boil. Turn down to a simmer (just bubbling) and cook for 20 minutes or until the water has disappeared. Leave to sit for 10 minutes and then fluff up with a fork.

2 In a pan saute the onion, oil, ginger and garlic for around 5 minutes or until the onion is clear.

3 Add the kumara and celery and cook for another 5 minutes or until soft.

4 Add remaining ingredients and mix gently.

5 Serve topped with lemon juice, red onion and fresh coriander.

THAI GREEN CURRY
JACKFRUIT & MILLET
TOSS AROUND

This is a lovely meal or accompaniment and includes fluffy millet which is a great alternative to rice, quinoa or couscous. Jackfruit is now available in many supermarkets in cans. It has a chicken-like texture. Out of the can it has a fruity taste, however, give it a good fry up and let it soak up some strong flavours and it will be transformed!

MAKES 4 X 1 CUP SERVES

1½ cups cooked millet (½ cup raw hulled millet and 1 cup boiling water)

400g (12oz) can young green jackfruit drained (around 1½ cups)

1 tablespoon oil

2 cloves garlic crushed or finely chopped

1 cup red onion (around 1 red onion) roughly diced

3 cups broccoli chopped small

1 tablespoon Thai green curry paste

1 tablespoon honey or date puree

½ teaspoon salt

garnish: fresh coriander (cilantro) chopped

1 Put millet and water in a pot. Place the lid on and bring to boil. Turn down to a simmer (just bubbling) and cook for 20 minutes or until the water has disappeared. Leave to sit for 10 minutes and then fluff up with a fork.

2 In a pot or pan saute the jackfruit and oil for 5 minutes until soft and starting to turn brown.

3 Use a wooden spoon to squash the jackfruit into smaller pieces and expose the fleshy texture.

4 Add the garlic and onion and saute for 5 minutes or until tender.

5 Add broccoli and cook for 3 minutes or until soft.

6 With a wooden spoon, move the ingredients to expose a corner of the pan. Add the curry paste, honey and salt. When hot and runny stir in.

7 Add the hot millet and stir through. Garnish with chopped coriander and serve immediately.

TIP Use hulled millet as the unhulled millet is very crunchy and will not cook to be light and fluffy.

ROASTED ALMOND &
BROCCOLI QUINOA
MINGLE

This simple mingle has a lovely texture. The crunchy roasted almonds are the hero of this dish.

MAKES 7 X 1 CUP SERVES

1½ cups cooked quinoa (½ cup raw quinoa and 1 cup boiling water)

1 cup onion finely diced (around 1 onion)

4 cloves garlic crushed or finely chopped

1 tablespoon oil

4 cups roughly chopped broccoli (around 1 large head)

1 teaspoon salt

2 cups frozen green peas

2 tablespoons Revive stock powder (page 123)

2 tablespoons water

garnish: ½ cup roasted almonds roughly chopped

1 Put quinoa and water in a pot. Place the lid on and bring to boil. Turn down to a simmer (just bubbling) and cook for 12 minutes or until the water has disappeared. Leave to sit for 10 minutes and then fluff up with a fork.

2 In a pot or pan saute the onion, garlic and oil for 5 minutes or until soft.

3 Add the broccoli and cook for a further 3 minutes.

4 Add the quinoa, salt and peas and cook for 5 more minutes or until all are hot and heated through.

5 Mix the stock powder with water and stir through the mingle.

6 Garnish with roasted almonds.

TIP If you only have raw almonds, roast in the oven for 10 minutes at 180°C (350°F). Slice on a chopping board with a sharp knife.

WARMING MIDDLE-OF-WINTER
KUMARA STIR FRY
WITH KALE AND BROCCOLI

Grated sweet potato is the key ingredient in this warming quick-to-make dish that gives awesome flavour and texture.

MAKES 5 X 1 CUP SERVES

1½ cups cooked quinoa (½ cup raw quinoa and 1 cup boiling water)

1 cup onion finely diced (around 1 onion)

3 cloves garlic crushed or finely chopped

1 tablespoon oil

3 cups grated orange kumara (sweet potato) (around 1 medium kumara)

4 cups boiling water

2 cups broccoli finely chopped

2 cups kale finely sliced

½ teaspoon salt

½ cup fresh coriander (cilantro) finely sliced

2 tablespoons lemon juice (around 1 lemon)

serve with: classic hummus (page 125)

1 Put quinoa and water in a pot. Place the lid on and bring to boil. Turn down to a simmer (just bubbling) and cook for 12 minutes or until the water has disappeared. Leave to sit for 10 minutes and then fluff up with a fork.

2 In a large pot or pan saute the onion, garlic and oil for 5 minutes or until soft.

3 Add the kumara and cook for another 5 minutes or until soft.

4 Prepare another pot with boiling water. Add the broccoli and kale. Cook for 3 minutes then drain.

5 To pan, with kumara, add the cooked quinoa, broccoli and kale. Sprinkle over the salt and coriander then stir in gently.

6 Drizzle lemon juice over the top and serve with a dollop of hummus.

TIP When cooking quinoa, cook extra and put it in the refrigerator as it makes a quick easy start stir fry for another time.

MAIN MEALS

KALE & TOFU RICOTTA
DEEP DISH PIZZA
WITH SWEET POTATO CRUST

MAKES 6 LARGE SLICES

1½ cups pizza sauce or all purpose tomato sauce (page 124)

garnish: lime & cashew aioli (page 122)

garnish: ¼ cup spring onions (scallions) sliced

SWEET POTATO CRUST

3 cups red kumara (sweet potato) diced, boiled and drained

¼ cup millet flour

¼ cup chickpea (chana/ besan) flour

2 tablespoons chia seeds

2 tablespoons olive oil

¼ teaspoon salt

KALE & TOFU RICOTTA FILLING

100g (3oz) kale (around 8 cups)

300g (10oz) firm tofu

4 tablespoons nutritional yeast flakes

½ teaspoon salt

1 cup onion finely diced (around 1 onion) sauteed

2 cloves garlic crushed or finely chopped

When I was in Chicago I saw a deep dish pizza which was essentially a dish full of melted cheese and it looked really really unhealthy. This is my real-food deep dish pizza full of awesome plant-powered ingredients!

1 Put the crust ingredients into a food processor and blend. Depending on the moisture in your kumara, you may need to add up to ½ cup of water to achieve a sticky dough.

2 Line a 27cm (11in) diameter round flan dish with baking (parchment) paper. Press the base mixture evenly into the bottom and up around the sides.

3 Bake at 180°C (350°F) for 20 minutes or until firm.

4 Blend filling ingredients in a food processor. Depending on moisture in your tofu, you may need to add up to ½ a cup of water.

5 Spoon pizza sauce onto base of the cooked pizza crust. Spoon kale filling on top.

6 Continue to bake for another 30 minutes at 180°C (350°F) or until firm. Baking time will vary depending on the size of your dish and the depth of the filling.

7 Let pizza cool for 10 minutes and then carefully lift out onto a wooden board. Cut into 6 wedges.

8 Garnish with aioli and spring onions.

CAULI & QUINOA BALLS
WITH MASALA GRAVY

These balls are a real hit in the cafes. They have a lovely texture and the masala sauce has amazing aroma and flavour!

MAKES 12 BALLS (6 SERVINGS)

BALLS

1½ cups cooked quinoa (½ cup raw quinoa and 1 cup boiling water)

2 cups cauliflower roughly chopped

½ cup fine rolled oats (quick-cook oats)

½ cup chickpea (chana/besan) flour

2 cloves garlic crushed or finely chopped

2 teaspoons cumin

1 teaspoon turmeric

¼ teaspoon chilli powder or cayenne

2 tablespoons honey or date puree

1 cup carrot grated (around ½ carrot)

1 teaspoon salt

MASALA GRAVY

2 teaspoons oil

1 cup onion finely diced (around 1 onion)

1 cup celery finely diced (around 1 stalk celery)

1 clove garlic

1 teaspoon cumin

1 teaspoon garam masala

1 teaspoon turmeric

1 teaspoon fennugreek powder

1 teaspoon salt

1 cup coconut cream

½ cup water

garnish: finely chopped parsley

1 Put quinoa and water in a pot. Place the lid on and bring to boil. Turn down to a simmer (just bubbling) and cook for 12 minutes or until the water has disappeared. Leave to sit for 10 minutes and then fluff up with a fork.

2 In a pot cook the cauliflower in boiling water for 5 minutes or until soft.

3 Mix all the balls ingredients in a large mixing bowl.

4 Line a baking tray with baking (parchment) paper.

5 Measure out ½ cup scoops of the ball mix, make them round in your hand and place on the tray.

6 Bake at 180°C (350°F) for 30 minutes or until firm and golden.

7 To make the masala gravy: In a pot or pan saute the oil, onion, celery and garlic for 5 minutes or until soft. Add the spices and salt and stir for 30 seconds to activate the flavour.

8 Stir in the coconut cream and water and heat (but do not boil).

9 Place the cooked balls in the pan of masala gravy to serve. Garnish with chopped parsley.

MELT IN YOUR MOUTH
GREEN VEGE CAKES
WITH SMOKY AIOLI

These are very popular and awesome way to get your green vegetables. They go amazingly with the smoky aioli!

MAKES 10 CAKES (5 SERVINGS)

1 teaspoon oil

2 cups grated courgette (zucchini) (around 2 large courgettes)

1 cup frozen peas

½ cup spring onion (scallions) finely sliced

1 cup chickpea (chana/besan) flour

½ cup water

½ cup fresh coriander (cilantro) finely chopped

½ cup mint finely chopped

100g (3oz) frozen spinach (defrosted in hot water) chopped

1 teaspoon salt

4 tablespoons sesame seeds

optional: up to 4 additional tablespoons of water

oil for frying

SMOKY AIOLI

¾ cups cashew nuts

½ clove garlic crushed or finely chopped

2 tablespoons lime juice (around 2 limes)

¼ cup water

2 teaspoons maple syrup

⅛ teaspoon salt

2 teaspoons smoked paprika

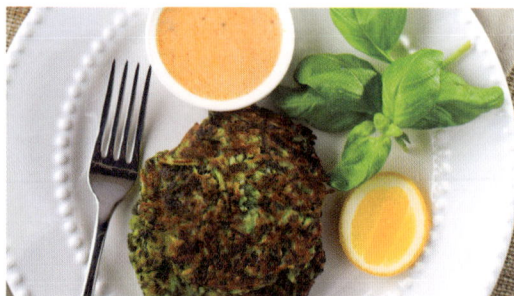

1 In a pot or pan saute the oil, courgette, peas and spring onion for 5 minutes or until soft.

2 In a mixing bowl add the chickpea flour and water. Stir until it forms a thick paste.

3 To the bowl add the remaining ingredients (except aioli) and the hot vegetable mix. You may need to add up 4 tablespoons extra of water to make a thick but pourable batter.

4 Heat a non-stick frying pan and add a little oil. Measure out ½ cup sized portions and drop in pan. Flatten down with a spatula.

5 Fry each side for 3 minutes or until golden brown and cooked inside.

6 Place the aioli ingredients into a blender and blend until smooth.

7 Serve vege cakes with aioli on the side.

TIP Having a good non-stick frying pan is critical so these cakes cook without breaking up.

MEXICAN SMOKED
JACKFRUIT TACOS
WITH LIME & CASHEW AIOLI

Very light, flavoursome and refreshing. Awesome summer lunch idea!

MAKES 6 TACOS

6 soft corn tacos

SMOKED JACKFRUIT FILLING

400g (12oz) can young green jackfruit drained (around 1½ cups)

2 teaspoons oil

1 cup onion finely diced (around 1 onion)

2 cloves garlic crushed or finely chopped

1 teaspoon smoked paprika

3 teaspoons tomato paste

3 tablespoons water

2 teaspoons maple syrup

½ teaspoon salt

TOPPINGS

¼ cup red cabbage sliced

½ cup cherry tomatoes sliced in half

1 avocado diced

¼ cup lime & cashew aioli dressing (page 122)

garnish: fresh coriander (cilantro) chopped

garnish: lime wedges

1 In a pot or pan saute the jackfruit, oil and onion and garlic for 10 minutes or until the jackfruit is broken apart and soft. Use a wooden spoon to press on the jackfruit and assist in breaking it up.

2 Add the smoked paprika and stir for 30 seconds to activate the flavour.

3 Add tomato paste, water, maple syrup and salt and stir until the jackfruit is well coated.

4 To heat and soften up the tacos, spray them with cold water and put in a hot non-stick frying pan for around 20 seconds each side.

5 Spoon the jackfruit filling onto the soft corn tacos. Add the toppings and garnishes.

TIP I have a spray bottle with water that works well for spraying tacos and freshening up lettuce.

ITALIAN
LEEK & ZUCCHINI PASTA
WITH PARMESHEW CHEESE

MAKES 4 X 1 CUP SERVES

4 cups leeks sliced (around 2 leeks)

2 cloves garlic crushed or finely chopped

2 cups courgettes (zucchini) sliced (around 2 courgettes

1 tablespoon oil

200g tube rice pasta (penne, rigatoni or tortiglioni)

boiling water

2 cups frozen peas

1 teaspoon salt

garnish: parsley finely chopped

garnish: lemon wedges

PARMESHEW CHEESE

2 tablespoons cashew nuts

2 tablespoons nutritional yeast flakes

Pasta is so quick and easy. Just add some flavoursome ingredients and a garnish, like this parmeshew cheese. Try some different pastas like rice or corn - they taste great and are usually healthier than refined wheat flour pastas.

1 In a pot or pan saute the leeks, garlic, courgettes and oil for 7 minutes or until soft.

2 In another pot cook the pasta according to packet directions in boiling water. Usually 8-10 minutes. Drain well.

3 Pour pasta into the pan with the leeks and stir. Add the peas and salt and gently combine. Stir for 2 minutes or until the peas have defrosted and warmed through.

4 Put parmeshew cheese ingredients into a blender and blend until fine.

5 Serve pasta garnished with parmeshew cheese, parsley and lemon wedges.

CRISPY
not-CHICKEN nuggets

MAKES 4 X ½ CUP SERVES

....

300g (10oz) firm tofu cut into 1½cm (½in) cubes

1 tablespoon soy sauce or tamari

oil spray

garnish: parsley chopped

serve with: lime & cashew aioli (page 122)

serve with: a healthy tomato sauce (ketchup)

garnish: parsley chopped

CRISPY COATING

2 tablespoons rice flour (white or brown)

½ teaspoon onion powder

¼ teaspoon garlic powder

½ teaspoon mixed herbs

½ teaspoon salt

2 tablespoons nutritional yeast flakes

These are awesome little nuggets and very easy to make. Kids love them.

....

1 Place tofu cubes into a bowl and pour over the soy sauce. Mix and leave to sit for 5 minutes.

2 Mix crispy coating ingredients in a shallow bowl.

3 Transfer the tofu cubes to the bowl containing the crispy coating ingredients. Coat evenly.

4 Line an oven tray with baking (parchment) paper and place the coated tofu cubes on it. Spray with oil spray.

5 Bake at 200°C (400°F) for 30 minutes or until golden brown, turning after 15 minutes.

6 Serve with aioli and/or tomato sauce and a light garnish of parsley.

TIP Keep leftover soy sauce in the refrigerator to use in a future meal like a stir fry.

FRESH AS LETTUCE
LENTIL TACOS
WITH HUMMUS & ARTICHOKES

MAKES 7 TACOS

....

1 large head of iceberg lettuce

LENTIL MIX

½ cup onion finely diced

1 clove garlic crushed or finely chopped

1 cup courgette (zucchini) finely diced (around 1 courgette)

1 tablespoon oil

400g (12oz) can brown lentils drained (around 1½ cups)

¼ teaspoon salt

TOPPINGS

1 cup artichoke hearts (small jar)

15 cherry tomatoes halved

½ avocado sliced

½ cup classic hummus (page 125)

¼ cup capers drained

garnish: fresh herbs or micro greens

These are so crunchy and tasty. Just roll them up when you are about to eat and munch on through the array of lovely flavours and textures.

....

1 In a pot or pan saute the onion, garlic, courgette and oil for 5 minutes or until soft.

2 Add the lentils and salt, then mix well. Leave to cool for 10 minutes.

3 Carefully peel off lettuce leaves to create cups.

4 Fill the lettuce cups with the warm lentil mixture and then add the toppings.

5 Garnish with fresh herbs or micro greens.

TIP This recipe is very flexible. Simply choose your favourite fillings to make them even more awesome!

ITALIAN CHICKPEA
BROCCOLI PIZZA
WITH SWEET POTATO

This pizza is very filling, nutritious and full of protein. Try this chickpea base instead of traditional white flour bases.

MAKES 6 SERVES (12 SLICES)

BASE

3 cups chickpea (chana/ besan) flour

3 cups water

1 teaspoon onion powder

½ teaspoon garlic powder

2 tablespoons oil

1 teaspoon salt

TOPPINGS

1 cup pizza sauce or all purpose tomato sauce (page 124)

½ cup red onion finely sliced and sauteed

2 cups broccoli finely chopped and steamed

2 cups orange kumara (sweet potato) diced and roasted

¼ cup kalamata olives (pitted)

¼ cup fresh coriander (cilantro) chopped

1 cup classic hummus (page 125)

1 In a mixing bowl, combine the chickpea flour with 1 cup of the water and mix well. Slowly add the rest of the water while mixing. This process will help avoid clumps of flour.

2 Add the onion powder, garlic powder, oil and salt then mix well.

3 Select an oven tray (with sides) around 300 x 400mm (12 x 16in). Place baking (parchment) paper on it.

4 Pour in the chickpea mix and bake at 180°C (350°F) for 15 minutes. The mixture may seem runny however this is normal and will be fine once cooked.

5 Remove the base from the oven. You can serve in the oven tray. Alternatively flip onto a chopping board, take the paper off, put another chopping board on top and flip around again.

6 Add toppings and serve immediately.

TIP The thickness of the pizza base is determined by the size of your oven tray. If it is large it will be thinner and crispier and require less cooking, if it is small it will be thicker, softer and therefore require more cooking.

TEMPEH & ROAST VEGE
RICE PAPER ROLLS

Try this delicious twist on the traditional Vietnamese rice paper rolls by using some roasted vegetables while keeping the same zingy flavour of the herbs.

MAKES 9 ROLLS

1 large parsnip sliced into strips

1 medium kumara (sweet potato) sliced into strips

oil spray

250g (8oz) block tempeh sliced into strips

1 tablespoon oil

½ red capsicum (bell pepper) finely sliced

1 cup red cabbage sliced

1 cup fresh herbs roughly chopped (mint, fresh coriander (cilantro), basil)

hot water

9 rice paper rolls 22cm (9 inch)

garnish: roasted peanuts chopped

QUICK SATAY SAUCE

4 tablespoons lemon juice

½ cup peanut butter

2 teaspoons honey or date puree

2 tablespoons water

1. Line a baking tray with baking (parchment) paper. Place the parsnip and kumara on and spray with oil. Bake at 200°C (400°F) for 30 minutes or until soft.

2. In a pan saute the tempeh with oil for 5 minutes per side or until golden brown. Remove and slice into thin long pieces.

3. Place all prepared vegetables and herbs onto a board.

4. Put some hot water into a large flat plate or bowl. Dip the rice paper sheet in the water for 10-15 seconds or until they are just softening. Place the rice paper sheet on the counter or chopping board.

5. Lay the ingredients in the center of the rice paper sheet. Fold in one end and wrap securely. Repeat with the remaining sheets.

6. In a blender, blend the quick satay sauce ingredients until smooth.

7. Garnish the rolls with chopped peanuts and mint. Serve with the satay sauce on the side.

SCRUMMY
MILLET LENTIL PATTIES

These patties make an awesome quick meal. Simply accompany with a fresh salad!

MAKES 20 PATTIES

1 cup onion finely diced (around 1 onion)

1 clove garlic crushed or finely chopped

1 teaspoon oil

1½ cup cooked millet (½ cup raw hulled millet and 1 cup boiling water)

400g (12oz) can brown lentils drained (around 1½ cups)

3 tablespoons chickpea (chana/besan) flour

½ cup water

1 teaspoon salt

2 tablespoons ground flaxseed (linseed) (purchase ground or grind with coffee grinder)

3 tablespoons almond butter

2 tablespoons soy sauce

oil for frying

garnish: chives finely sliced

1 Put millet and water in a pot. Place the lid on and bring to a boil. Turn down to a simmer (just bubbling) and cook for 20 minutes or until the water has disappeared. Leave to sit for 10 minutes and then fluff up with a fork.

2 In a pot or pan saute the onion, garlic and oil for 5 minutes or until soft.

3 In a large mixing bowl combine all ingredients and stir well.

4 Heat a non-stick pan. Add 1 teaspoon of oil per batch of 6 patties.

5 Spoon heaped tablespoons of the pattie mix into the pan and flatten with a spatula. Cook for 2 minutes each side or until cooked through and golden brown.

TIP Instead of millet you could use rice, quinoa or couscous.

BUCKWHEAT &
SPINACH CREPES
WITH CASHEW SOUR CREAM

I love these crepes. They are scrummy and are so easy to make.

MAKES 6 CREPES

1 cup water

1 tablespoon lemon juice

1 tablespoon oil

1 clove garlic crushed or finely chopped

6 cups fresh spinach or 200g (6oz) frozen spinach defrosted

¾ cup buckwheat flour

½ teaspoon salt

oil for frying

garnish: cherry tomatoes

garnish: green frozen peas (defrosted in hot water)

garnish: fresh mint leaves

garnish: salt

CASHEW SOUR CREAM

¾ cups cashews

6 tablespoons water

2 tablespoons lemon juice

⅛ teaspoon salt

1 Blend all ingredients in a food processor until smooth.

2 Put a little oil in a non-stick frying pan. Pour in a thin layer of batter and cook each side for 3 minutes or until golden.

3 Blend cashew sour cream ingredients in a blender until smooth.

4 Serve garnished with cherry tomatoes, green peas, mint, cashew sour cream and salt.

TIP You need a good non-stick frying pan to make these pancakes, or they may stick.

THAI GREEN CURRY
TOFU STEAKS

MAKES 12 STEAKS

....

600g (18oz) firm tofu sliced into slabs around 1cm (½in) thick

1 tablespoon oil

3 tablespoons Thai green curry paste

3 tablespoons maple syrup

¾ teaspoon salt

2 tablespoons lemon juice (around 1 lemon)

garnish: coriander (cilantro)

garnish: lime wedges

An awesome protein accompaniment or feature part of a main meal.

....

1   In a non-stick frying pan saute the tofu and oil for 5 minutes or until the water has evaporated and the tofu is chewy.

2   In a bowl mix together the curry paste, maple syrup, salt and lemon juice. Pour over the tofu.

3   Cook tofu for another 5 minutes or until browned. Turn every couple of minutes. Be careful not to burn the tofu.

4   Serve with coriander and lime wedges.

TIP   This tofu is excellent cold so make extra to store in the refrigerator for a meal the next day.

NACHOS
WITH NACHO CHEESE SAUCE & GUACAMOLE

Who does not like nachos? You will not be disappointed with the flavour and texture of this healthy nacho cheese sauce.

MAKES 4 SERVES

4 cups nacho cheese sauce (page 144)

200g natural corn chips (without flavour enhancers)

200g (6oz) cherry tomatoes mixed colours cut in half

1 green capsicum (bell pepper) finely diced

garnish: coriander (cilantro)

QUICK GUACAMOLE

1 large avocado

1 tablespoon lemon juice

¼ teaspoon salt

1 Make nacho cheese sauce as per recipe.

2 Place corn chips on a plate. Pour over the nacho cheese sauce and sprinkle vegetables on top.

3 Use a fork to mash and mix guacamole ingredients in a bowl. Put a dollop on each plate.

4 Garnish with coriander.

TIP The corn chips will soak up the nacho cheese sauce, so make sure you serve straight away. Alternatively put the ingredients on the table for your friends and family to assemble themselves.

HAWAIIAN
POKE BOWL
WITH JAPANESE WASABI DRESSING

A poke bowl (pronounced poke-eh) is usually found in Hawaii and traditionally consists of raw fish, vegetables and dressings. There are now many poke bars popping up around the world. Here is my plant-based version. In preparing for the shoot I had a poke party with some friends, where everyone could customise their own poke bowl.

MAKES 2 BOWLS

1 cup cooked brown rice (½ cup raw long grain brown rice and 1 cup boiling water)

300g (10oz) tofu

¼ teaspoon salt

2 teaspoons oil

1 cup edamame (usually purchased frozen) defrosted in hot water

1 cup courgettes (zucchini) spiralised (or julienne)

½ cup carrots julienned

½ cup red cabbage finely sliced

¼ cup radish finely sliced

½ avocado diced

optional: fried shallots

¼ cup Japanese wasabi dressing (page 121)

garnish: fresh coriander (cilantro) finely chopped

garnish: black & white sesame seeds

1 Put rice and water in a pot. Place the lid on and bring to boil. Turn down to a simmer (just bubbling) and cook for 25 minutes or until the water has disappeared. Leave to sit for 10 minutes and then fluff up with a fork.

2 In a pot or pan saute the tofu, salt and oil for 10 minutes or until the tofu is golden and chewy.

3 Place all the prepared vegetables onto a chopping board or plate.

4 Cluster the ingredients in serving bowls. Drizzle the dressing over and add garnishes.

TIP This dish is most authentic when using chopsticks if you can manage it!

SIDES & FLAVOUR BOOSTERS

CRISPY CRUNCHY OVEN BAKED
POLENTA FRIES

Try these lovely crunchy polenta chips for something a little different. A chef friend of mine told me that most polenta chips in restaurants have a lot of butter and cheese and are often double deep fried. So enjoy these healthy, but still tasty ones!

MAKES 6 SERVES

2½ cups boiling water

4 tablespoons Revive stock powder (page 123)

1 tablespoon oil

1 cup fine polenta (cornmeal)

½ cup coarse polenta (cornmeal)

oil spray or oil

garnish: chopped parsley

garnish: salt

1 Put boiling water, stock powder and olive oil into a pot and heat until it is back to a boil (bubbling).

2 While stirring, add the fine polenta and stir well. Turn heat down and stir for 3 minutes or until mixture is thick.

3 Line a small cake tin 20cm x 20cm (8in x 8in) with baking (parchment) paper. Pour the mixture in and spread evenly.

4 Put the tin in the freezer for 30 minutes to set the polenta.

5 Place upside down on a chopping board, remove the paper, and slice into chip sized pieces around 1cm (½in) thick.

6 Spread the coarse polenta on a plate. Roll the chips in the coarse polenta and place on a baking tray lined with baking (parchment) paper.

7 Spray lightly with oil spray or brush over with oil. Bake at 200°C (400°F) for 40 minutes or until firm and golden.

8 Serve immediately with a garnish of parsley and salt.

ENERGISING
CAULI & BROCCOLI
RICE

This is an incredibly tasty alternative to rice or quinoa to have underneath a curry or liquidy type dish. It is so healthy, fresh and flavoursome and it is faster to cook! Can also be served as a side dish.

MAKES 5 X 1 CUP SERVES

3 cups broccoli florets (around 1 small head of broccoli)

3 cups cauliflower florets (around ¼ medium cauliflower)

1 tablespoon oil

½ teaspoon salt

garnish: lime slices

1 Place broccoli and cauliflower florets in a food processor and process until you have a rice-sized pieces and texture.

TIP It is important not to over process or you will end up with slush. There are usually a couple of naughty pieces that refuse to cut up so I empty the mix out, and re-process these larger pieces separately.

2 In a pot or pan combine all the ingredients and lightly stir-fry for 5 minutes or until the "rice" has just softened.

3 Serve immediately. You can add an optional squeeze of lime juice to taste.

TIP If you do not have a food processor or do not want to get it dirty, you can prepare this dish by using a hand grater to process the broccoli and cauliflower.

BRILLIANTLY SCRUMMY
SALMON-LIKE BITES
WITH CASHEW CREAM CHEESE

MAKES 10 SMALL SERVES

4 cups peeled carrot (around 2 very large carrots)

1½ tablespoon olive oil

½ teaspoon smoked paprika

¼ teaspoon salt

serve with: 2 slices rye or pumpernickel bread (cut into quarters)

serve with: cashew cream cheese (page 150)

garnish: chives finely sliced

These are excellent appetisers - they are unique and very very tasty.

1 Peel the outside of the carrots as you normally would and discard peelings.

2 Then peel the carrots completely with the peeler so you get wide and fine shreds of carrot. Place into a bowl.

3 To the bowl add the olive oil, smoked paprika and salt and mix thoroughly but gently, so you do not damage the carrot peels.

4 Take an oven tray and line with baking (parchment) paper. Place the carrot on the tray so there is minimal overlapping.

5 Bake at 180°C (350°F) for 15 minutes or until the carrot is soft but not breaking apart.

6 Serve on rye or pumpernickel bread with cashew cream cheese and a garnish of chives.

BANGKOK GOOEY
PEANUTY SATAY
TOFU CHUNKS

This satay sauce is so easy to make. It goes amazingly well with the traditionally bland tofu as the tofu just soaks up all the flavours.

MAKES 4 X 1 CUP SERVES

600g (20 oz) firm tofu drained and cubed

1 tablespoon oil

garnish: chopped fresh coriander (cilantro)

SATAY SAUCE

1 tablespoon Thai red curry paste

1 tablespoon ginger puree or ginger finely chopped

2 tablespoons smooth peanut butter

2 tablespoons lemon juice

1 tablespoon maple syrup

¼ cup hot water

½ teaspoon salt

1 In a pan cook the tofu and oil for 10 minutes or until it is golden brown. Depending on the firmness and water in your tofu this step may take between 5 and 15 minutes.

2 Set the tofu aside. In the hot pan put the satay sauce ingredients and stir around for 2 minutes or until you have a nice smooth sauce. You may need to add a little more water.

3 Combine the tofu with the sauce. Cook for 5 minutes or until the flavours have soaked in and the tofu is well coated and starts to caramalise.

4 Serve with a garnish of chopped fresh coriander.

GINGER & GARLIC INFUSED
SAUTEED SPINACH
MINGLE

Spinach gets a bad rap for being boring and bland. This is a lovely side dish that is so simple yet bursting with flavour and freshness.

MAKES 4 X 1 CUP SERVES

1 cup onion finely diced (around 1 onion)

1 teaspoon oil

1 tablespoon ginger puree or ginger finely chopped

2 cloves garlic crushed or finely chopped

200g (6oz) (a large bunch) of fresh spinach

½ teaspoon salt

1 tablespoon olive oil

garnish: 1 lemon

1 In a pan saute the onion, oil, ginger and garlic for around 5 minutes or until the onion is clear.

2 Prepare the spinach by washing well and slicing. The stalks are tasty so include these, although it is important they are sliced very thin.

3 Add the spinach and salt and let it wilt for 2 minutes.

4 Drizzle olive oil over the top and mix gently.

5 Serve immediately with lemon as a garnish to squeeze over as desired.

TIP Embrace the stalks! Don't throw them away, simply chop them up finely - they add great texture!

A LITTLE BIT OF
FANCY QUINOA
ON THE SIDE

Quinoa is a great accompaniment for curries and casseroles. However, why not make it more special. This supercharged version has amazing flavours and is enhanced even more with my crumbly plant-powered feta cheese!

MAKES 4 X 1 CUP SERVES

3 cups cooked quinoa (1 cup raw quinoa and 2 cups boiling water)

1 cup onion finely diced (around 1 onion)

2 cloves garlic crushed or finely chopped

1 tablespoon oil

1 cup frozen green peas

½ teaspoon salt

¼ cup fresh coriander (cilantro) stalks finely diced

garnish: crumbly tofu feta (page 148)

1 Put quinoa and water in a pot. Place the lid on and bring to boil. Turn down to a simmer (just bubbling) and cook for 12 minutes or until the water has disappeared. Leave to sit for 10 minutes and then fluff up with a fork.

2 In a pot or pan saute the onion, garlic and oil for 5 minutes or until soft.

3 Add the cooked quinoa, peas, salt and fresh coriander and cook for 3 minutes or until the ingredients are heated through and the peas have defrosted.

4 Serve with a garnish of crumbled feta.

CRUNCHY THYME & CARROT CRACKERS
SERVED WITH BASIL RICOTTA CHEESE

Make your own crackers! This is another simple "throw all the ingredients into a food processor" recipe. You can make them crunchy by cooking longer, or softer by cooking less.

MAKES AROUND 30 CRACKERS

½ cup cashew nuts

¼ cup whole flaxseed (linseed)

¾ cup ground flaxseed (linseed) (purchase ground or grind with coffee grinder)

4 cups grated carrot (around 3 large carrots)

¼ cup water

¼ cup nutritional yeast

1 tablespoons dried thyme or ¼ cup fresh chopped thyme

1 teaspoon salt

serve with: basil ricotta cheese (page 151)

1 Add cashews to a food processor and blend until powdered.

2 Add remaining ingredients to food processor and process until mixed. Note this recipe will not work in a blender (liquidiser).

3 Put baking (parchment) paper on a baking tray. Spoon out the mixture onto the tray and press down evenly with a spatula to 3mm (⅛in)thickness. Try to spread as evenly as possible.

4 Using a knife, score into 4cm (2in) squares.

5 Bake at 120°C (250°F) for 60-90 minutes or until crunchy in texture. If the crackers are still chewy, cook a little longer.

6 Let cool. Serve with basil ricotta cheese, hummus or your favourite dip.

TIP Can be stored in an airtight container for about a week. If the crackers soften, simply heat in the oven to remove the moisture.

TIP This recipe uses a lower than usual oven temperature to dry the crackers out rather than cook them.

REVIVE
Cucumber RAITA
with mint

A great plant-powered alternative to the yogurt-based version. Great on curries, especially when they are hot!

MAKES 3 CUPS

1 cup cashews

2 cups boiling water (to soak)

150g (5oz) firm tofu (around half a block)

4 tablespoons lemon juice (around 2 lemons)

¼ cup cold water

1 teaspoon salt

2 cups grated cucumber (around 1 medium cucumber)

½ cup mint roughly chopped (reserve some mint for garnish)

1 Soak cashews in boiling water for 10 minutes to soften them. Drain and discard water.

2 Place cashews, tofu, lemon juice, cold water and salt into a blender and blend until very smooth and silky. If there are gritty bits, let it sit to soak for 10 minutes and blend again.

3 Pour into a bowl and gently mix in the cucumber and mint.

4 Garnish with reserved mint.

TIP This raita is best served on the day it is made.

JAPANESE
WASABI DRESSING

This is a lovely creamy dressing bursting with maple and wasabi flavours. It is a great example of how to add some simple flavours to a transform a basic dressing into something incredible.

MAKES 1 CUP

½ cup Brazil nuts (you can also use cashews or almonds)

4 tablespoons lemon juice (around 2 lemons)

½ teaspoon salt

2 teaspoons wasabi paste

½ cup water

2 teaspoons maple syrup

¼ cup fresh coriander (cilantro) chopped

1   Place Brazil nuts into a blender and blend until they are powder.

2   Add remaining ingredients into the blender and blend for 30 seconds or until smooth.

TIP   If dressing is too thick add a little water. If your dressing is too watery add more nuts and re-blend. If dressing is not creamy, wait 10 minutes and re-blend after it has had some time to soak.

SIMPLE BUT EXTREMELY DELICIOUS
LIME & CASHEW AIOLI

This is our "go to" dressing at Revive and can be used across many dishes.

MAKES 2 CUPS

1½ cups cashew nuts

1½ cups boiling water (to soak)

1 clove garlic crushed or finely chopped

4 tablespoons lime juice (around 4 limes)

¾ cup cold water

1 tablespoon maple syrup

¼ teaspoon salt

1 Soak cashew nuts in boiling water for 10 minutes. Drain.

2 Place softened cashews and remaining ingredients into a blender. Blend until smooth and creamy.

3 If needed add a little water to achieve the perfect silky consistency.

TIP Some blenders struggle with a small volume. You can use a stick blender or double the recipe to make it work.

REVIVE STOCK
POWDER

This is an excellent general purpose healthy stock. It can be used directly in soups and curries or mixed with water before stirring in. It is most similar to a chicken type stock. Most stocks contain flavour enhancers and highly modified fats. This recipe makes a much healthier version.

MAKES 1½ CUPS

¾ cup nutritional yeast flakes

1 tablespoon salt

1 teaspoon turmeric

2 tablespoons coconut sugar

2 tablespoons onion powder

1 teaspoon celery seeds

1 tablespoon rice flour

1 teaspoon paprika

1   Mix all ingredients together in a bowl.

2   Transfer to an airtight container.

TIP   Will keep in an airtight container for around 2 months.

ALL PURPOSE
TOMATO SAUCE

We use this tomato sauce for lasagnas, pizzas and any other time that
we need a great tasting tomato base.

MAKES 6 CUPS

1½ cups onion chopped (around
1 onion)

4 cloves garlic crushed

2 tablespoons oil

3 x 400g (12oz) cans tomatoes

¾ teaspoon salt

1 teaspoon mixed dried herbs

3 tablespoons honey or date puree

1 In a pot or pan saute onion, garlic and
oil for 5 minutes or until soft.

2 Add remaining ingredients and cook
for 4 minutes or until bubbling.

3 Blend the sauce with a stick blender.

TIP If you really love garlic, add
twice as much for a great
garlic taste.

CLASSIC
Hummus

This is a great hummus recipe that goes with so many dishes.

MAKES 3 CUPS

2 x 400g (12oz) cans chickpeas (garbanzo beans) drained (around 3 cups)

½ teaspoon of salt

2 cloves of garlic chopped or crushed

2 tablespoons tahini (ground hulled sesame seed paste)

½ cup water

4 tablespoons lemon juice

1 Put all ingredients in food processor and blend until smooth. You can also use a stick blender or a regular blender however you may have to add more water to keep it flowing.

2 Taste. Note that all batches vary in flavour as garlic, chickpeas and lemon juice often have different flavours and consistency.

3 Add extra water/salt/lemon juice/ garlic as needed. You should be able to taste every ingredient slightly, with not too much of any ingredient dominating the hummus.

VEGAN CHEESES

VEGAN CHEESES
NOTES

I hope you enjoy making these lovely cheese recipes. We have spent many hours developing and making these recipes as bullet proof as possible.

It is important that you follow the recipe methods closely in order to have the best possible outcome.

Some of the ingredients can vary depending on where they are purchased so some recipes may need adjusting.

AGAR AGAR POWDER

This is made from seaweed! While it can be purchase in strips to blend at home, I recommend you purchase the powdered variety. It is available in most Asian stores and some health stores. When using please take note of the cooking times and methods within each recipe. It is important that the agar agar powder is properly activated by heating which is what enables it to form a thick gel.

CASHEW NUTS & ALMONDS

These add thickening, mouth-feel and flavour. They need to be soaked and well blended so they become smooth and creamy. The recipes that use these nuts start with soaking them in boiling water for 10 minutes to make them soft. If you find small nut pieces after blending, leave the mixture to sit for 10 minutes to soak further then blend again.

COCONUT OIL

Coconut oil is solid when cold so it is a good addition to vegan cheeses. However it needs to be warmed up to become liquid and mix properly. You can add while solid if you are adding to a hot mixture as it will melt quickly.

NUTRITIONAL YEAST FLAKES

Nutritional yeast flakes (sometimes called savoury yeast flakes) are available at health stores and some grocery stores. These flakes give a lovely cheesy, salty flavour. They often come in different strengths so you may need to adjust the amount used to achieve the desired flavour in your cheese.

TAPIOCA STARCH (FLOUR)

This is a great thickening agent made from cassava root. I have found it often labelled with the name "arrowroot" (which is made from a different plant) however the packaging shows the contents as tapioca starch and this is fine to use. In my experience "true" arrowroot will not work as well.

BLENDER

You need a powerful blender for some of the recipes to ensure the ingredients are well blended for a smooth texture.

SAUCEPAN

For recipes that call for cooking, use a heavy based saucepan or frying pan (ideally non-stick) and stir well with a wooden spoon to avoid burning.

CHILLING

Many of the cheeses start out being cooked and then need to be chilled so that they set. I recommend using a freezer as this will make the setting process significantly faster. It is important that you remove the cheese from the freezer when it is set and transfer it to the refrigerator to store. If you keep freezing, it will develop ice crystals which will change the texture of the cheese, in a bad way. I recommend setting an alarm or timer so you do not forget. Alternatively if you are not under time pressure, you can put in the cheese in the refrigerator and wait longer for it to set.

SCALABILITY

All of the cheese recipes are easily scalable. Simply double or triple the recipe and use larger setting containers. The setting times may increase slightly.

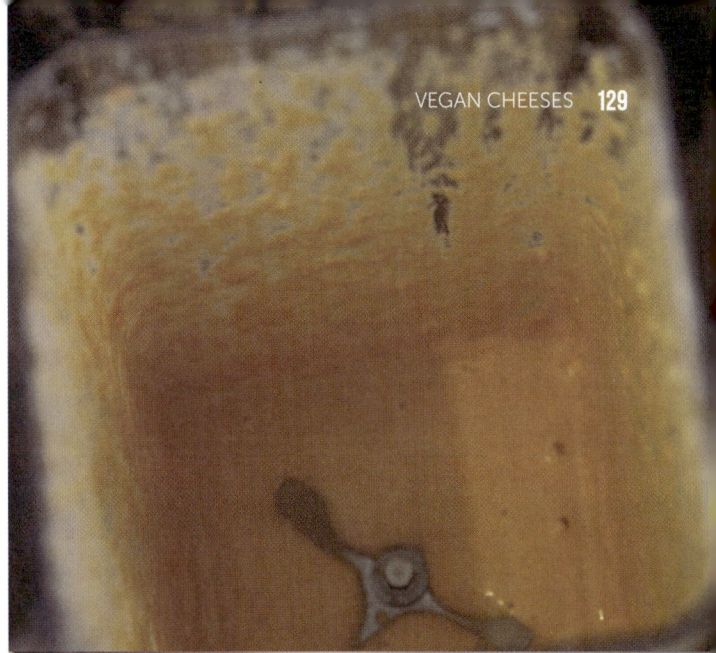

CASHEW
CHEDDAR CHEESE

This is a great tasting all purpose cheese for toasted sandwiches, salads, crackers and even on lasagnes. You will love the flavour and texture!

MAKES 1 BLOCK (1¼ CUPS)

½ cup cashew nuts

1 cup boiling water (to soak)

1½ teaspoons tapioca starch (flour)

2 tablespoons nutritional yeast flakes

2 tablespoons lemon juice (around 1 lemon)

½ teaspoon salt

¼ cup grated carrot (around ½ large carrot)

¼ teaspoon mustard powder

¼ cup hot water

2 tablespoons coconut oil (melted)

½ cup cold water

2 teaspoons agar agar powder

1 Soak cashew nuts in a bowl of boiling water for 10 minutes to soften. Drain.

2 Place the soaked cashew nuts in a blender. Add tapioca starch, nutritional yeast flakes, lemon juice, salt, carrot, mustard powder, ¼ cup of hot water and coconut oil and blend until smooth.

3 In a pot mix ½ cup of cold water and agar agar powder and bring to the boil while stirring. Cook and stir for 2 more minutes to activate the agar agar powder.

4 Add the blended cashew mixture to the agar pot while stirring. Cook for a further 2 minutes stirring continuously.

5 Lightly oil a small rectangular dish and pour in the cooked cheese mix. Place in the freezer for 30 minutes to set. After this store in the refrigerator.

6 Take out of the freezer and bang upside down on a bread board to release the cheese. You may need to use a knife to assist. Slice and grate just like normal cheese!

TIP Store covered in the refrigerator for 2 days.

ENTERTAINING WORTHY
HERBY CASHEW CHEESE

Awesome vegan alternative that holds its own on a cheese board. This recipe also works well with fresh coriander (cilantro), mint and chives.

MAKES 1 ROUND

½ cup cashew nuts

1 cup boiling water (to soak)

1½ teaspoons tapioca starch (flour)

1 cloves garlic crushed or finely chopped

3 tablespoons nutritional yeast flakes

1 tablespoon lemon juice (around ½ lemon)

½ teaspoon salt

½ cup chopped Italian parsley

2 tablespoons chopped fresh thyme

½ cup cold water

1½ teaspoons agar agar powder

garnish: ½ cup finely chopped Italian parsley

1 Soak cashew nuts in a bowl of boiling water for 10 minutes to soften. Drain.

2 Add the soaked cashew nuts, tapioca starch, garlic, nutritional yeast, lemon juice and salt in a blender and blend until very smooth.

3 Add parsley and thyme to blender and pulse for a few seconds until mixed through in little pieces.

TIP Be careful not to blend herbs too long as you will end up with a green cheese instead of green pieces in white cheese.

4 In a pot mix cold water and agar agar powder. Pour in the cashew mix and bring to the boil while stirring. Cook for another 2 minutes stirring constantly.

5 Pour into a lightly oiled round dish and put in freezer for 30 minutes or until firm. After this store in the refrigerator.

6 Take out and bang upside down on chopping board to release. Press chopped parsley into the cheese with your hands.

7 Store in the refrigerator for around 2 days.

CASHEW-POWERED
GRILLED HALLOUMI

Halloumi is a lovely salty cheese that grills up wonderfully with a soft inside and crispy exterior. This cashew-powered version is a pretty good as a healthy knock-off and tastes awesome!

MAKES 10-14 SLICES

1 cup cashew nuts

2 cups boiling water (to soak)

1 cup cold water

4 tablespoons tapioca starch (flour)

1 tablespoon agar agar powder

2 tablespoons coconut oil

1½ teaspoons salt

oil for frying

1 Place cashew nuts into a bowl with the boiling water and leave for 10 minutes to soften. Drain.

2 To a blender add the soaked cashew nuts and all other ingredients (except oil for frying). Blend until smooth.

3 Pour the blended cashew mixture into a pot and slowly heat, stirring constantly as it thickens.

4 Continue stirring until the mixture clumps together. While stirring, cook for another 2 minutes to activate the agar agar powder.

5 Transfer to a dish lined with baking (parchment) paper. Ideally the depth will be 2 cm (just under 1 inch). Flatten the mixture.

6 Put in the freezer for 30 minutes. After this time store in the refrigerator if not frying immediately.

7 Remove from dish and put halloumi onto a chopping board and cut into thin slices.

8 In a non-stick frying pan add some oil and fry the halloumi slices for 3 minutes each side or until brown and crispy.

TIP Use a textured grill if you want grill lines on your cheese.

PLANT-POWERED
MOZZARELLA BALLS
WITH LEMON & GARLIC

This is a lovely mozzarella cheese that is great in salads and on pizzas!

·····································

MAKES 12-15 BALLS

·····································

1 cup cashew nuts

1 cup boiling water (to soak)

1 cup almond milk (unsweetened)

3 tablespoons tapioca starch (flour)

1 tablespoon agar agar powder

¼ teaspoon citric acid

1 teaspoon salt

6 cups cold water

3 cups ice cubes

MARINADE (OPTIONAL)

1 tablespoon lemon zest

2 cloves garlic crushed or finely chopped

½ cup olive oil

1 Place cashew nuts into a bowl with the boiling water and leave for 10 minutes to soften. Drain.

2 Place soaked cashew nuts and all ingredients (except the ice cold water and ice cubes), into a blender and blend until smooth.

3 Pour blended mixture into a pot and slowly heat, stirring constantly until it bubbles. Keep stirring until mixture clumps together.

4 Cook for a further 2 minutes, while stirring, to ensure agar agar powder is activated. You should end up with a sticky bread dough-like texture.

5 Put the cold water and ice cubes into a bowl.

6 Scoop out balls (around 2 tablespoons in size) from the pot with a spoon and use another spoon to scrape balls off into the iced water.

7 Leave the balls to sit in the iced water for 10 minutes to firm up.

TIP You can use immediately or marinate in a jar with the marinade ingredients. Leave in the refrigerator overnight.

SMOOTH & VERSATILE
CHICKPEA PANEER

This is a great alternative to dairy paneer found in Indian cooking. Using chickpea flour, this great cheese-like substance is awesome in salads and Indian curries.

MAKES 2 CUPS

1¾ cups cold water

1 cup chickpea (chana/ besan) flour

2 tablespoons Revive stock powder (page 123)

1 tablespoon oil

½ teaspoon salt

1 tablespoon oil for sauteing

1 Place water, chickpea flour, stock, oil and salt into a blender. Blend until smooth.

2 Pour into a pot and heat the mixture stirring regularly until it is bubbling. Cook while stirring for another 2 minutes until it thickens.

3 Place the chickpea mixture onto a baking tray lined with baking (parchment) paper. Smooth over with a spatula so it is 1cm (½in) deep.

4 Place in the freezer for 30 minutes or until firm.

5 Place upside down on a chopping board, remove paper and cut into 1cm (½in) cubes with a sharp knife.

6 In a pot or pan saute the cubes in oil for 5 minutes or until golden.

VEGAN VERY GRATEABLE CHEESE

MAKES 1½ CUP BLOCK
MAKES 2-3 CUPS GRATED

....

1½ cups almond milk (unsweetened)

1½ tablespoons agar agar powder

2 tablespoons coconut oil

1½ tablespoons tapioca starch (flour)

1½ tablespoons chickpea (chana/besan) flour

2 tablespoons nutritional yeast flakes

1½ tablespoons lemon juice (around ¾ lemon)

1 teaspoon salt

You will love the texture of this cheese. It is the firmest of all my cheeses which makes it ideal for grating. You can grate it thick, medium or angel hair size. Or simply slice like dairy cheese.

....

1 Mix the milk and agar agar powder in a pot and bring to the boil while stirring. Turn down and let bubble gently while stirring for 4 minutes to activate the agar agar.

2 In a bowl measure out the remaining ingredients. This is to facilitate a quick transfer.

3 Put the hot agar mixture in a blender. Add the measured out ingredients. Blend for 30 seconds or until thoroughly mixed and becomes a silky smooth texture.

4 Pour the mixture into a small rectangular dish.

TIP This cheese sets quickly so work fast to get it into the bowl to start setting.

5 Place in the freezer for 15 minutes to set. Keep in the refrigerator after this time.

CREAMY VEGAN
GOUDA CHEESE

A lovely mild and silky cheese - awesome on crackers and cheese boards.

MAKES 1 BLOCK

½ cup almond milk (unsweetened)

4 tablespoons tapioca starch (flour)

1½ tablespoons chickpea (chana/besan) flour

2 tablespoons nutritional yeast flakes

2 tablespoons olive oil

1 tablespoon lemon juice (around ½ lemon)

1 teaspoon apple cider vinegar

½ teaspoon salt

1 cup almond milk (unsweetened)

3 teaspoons agar agar powder

1 Put all ingredients (except final almond milk and agar agar powder) in a blender and blend until smooth.

2 In a pot mix the 1 cup of almond milk with the agar agar powder and bring to a boil while stirring. Turn the heat down to medium and let it simmer for a further 2 minutes while stirring to activate the agar agar powder.

3 Slowly pour in the blended mixture into the pot. Cook for a further 3 minutes while stirring.

4 Rub some oil in a small dish and pour the mixture in.

5 Place in the freezer for 30 minutes or until firm. After this store in the refrigerator.

CAN'T BELIEVE IT'S NOT CHEESE

NACHO CHEESE SAUCE

This is a lovely silky smooth and cheesy nacho sauce that you will not believe is made from potatoes and carrots!

MAKES 4 X 1 CUP SERVES

2 cups diced potatoes (around 2 medium potatoes)

2 cups diced carrots (around 2 medium carrots)

½ cup onion finely diced (around ½ onion)

2 cloves garlic crushed or finely chopped

1½ cups cooking water from the vegetables

400g (12oz) can butter (lima) beans drained (around 1½ cups)

½ cup nutritional yeast flakes

2 tablespoons oil

¼ cup tapioca starch (flour)

2 tablespoons seeded (wholegrain) mustard

1 tablespoon lemon juice (around ½ lemon)

1½ teaspoons salt

1 Put the potatoes, carrots, onion and garlic into a pot and cover with boiling water. Cook for 15 minutes or until soft.

2 Drain and save the water.

3 Place all ingredients into a food processor and blend until smooth.

4 Pour mixture into a pot or pan and heat gently, stirring for 5 minutes or until it thickens. You may need to add a little more water to achieve a pourable yet thick consistency.

VEGAN
MARINATED FETA
CHEESE

MAKES 2 CUPS

300g (10oz) firm or pressed tofu

MARINADE

¼ cup lemon juice (around 2 lemons)

1 teaspoon apple cider vinegar

¼ cup water

2 tablespoon olive oil

1½ teaspoons nutritional yeast flakes

½ teaspoon dried mixed herbs

1 clove garlic crushed or finely chopped

¼ teaspoon salt

This is a great plant-powered feta substitute and it is so easy. It is just pressed tofu with a very simple marinade!

1   If you have very firm or pressed tofu you do not have to do this step. Press the Tofu: Use a tofu press or simply place between 2 chopping boards. Put a heavy weight on top to assist. It helps to put the boards on a slight lean into the sink so the water drains into it. This process takes around 30 minutes. Pressing will not work with silken or soft tofu.

2   Mix all marinade ingredients together in a jar.

3   Slice the tofu into 1cm (½in) cubes. Add the pressed tofu to the jar and shake gently.

4   Refrigerate and let flavours mingle for around 3 hours or overnight before using.

TIP   Keep refrigerated and use within 3 days.

LIGHT & CRUMBLY
TOFU FETA CHEESE

This is a great version of feta that is useful for crumbling through salads or over main dishes like lasagnes.

....

MAKES 2 CUPS

....

300g (12oz) very firm or pressed tofu (around 1 block)

3 tablespoons coconut oil (melted)

3 tablespoons lemon juice (around 1½ lemons)

½ teaspoon salt

1 If tofu is not pressed, place a weight on it for 15-30 minutes to press out as much water as you can.

2 Place all ingredients into a blender and blend until smooth. You may need to press the mixture down to assist.

3 Pour into a small dish lined with baking (parchment) paper.

4 Cover with plastic wrap and place in freezer for 30 minutes. Keep in the refrigerator after this time.

5 Remove from the dish and crumble or slice as needed. Will keep for around 3 days.

SWEET
ALMOND RICOTTA

This is great for sweet recipes like with toast, fruit or desserts.

MAKES 2 CUPS

1 cup slivered almonds or 1½ cups blanched (without skin) almonds

2 cups boiling water (to soak)

¾ cup cold water

⅛ teaspoon salt

1 tablespoon maple syrup

1 tablespoon lemon juice

1 Place almonds into a bowl with the boiling water and leave for 10 minutes to soften. Drain.

2 Put the soaked almonds and all remaining ingredients into a blender and blend until creamy.

3 Will keep for 2 days in the refrigerator.

CASHEW
CREAM CHEESE

A lovely cheese for crackers and where you would normally use cream cheese,

MAKES 2 CUPS

1 teaspoon agar agar powder

½ cup cold water

1 cup cashew nuts

1 cup sunflower seeds

2 cups boiling water (to soak)

1 clove garlic crushed or finely chopped

1 teaspoon salt

1 tablespoon lemon juice

1 Make agar agar gel: Put the agar agar powder and cold water into a pot or pan and heat while stirring until bubbling. Continue to cook for 2 minutes while stirring to activate the agar agar.

2 Put cashew nuts, sunflower seeds and boiling water into a bowl and let sit for 10 minutes to soak. Drain.

3 Transfer the soaked cashew nuts and sunflower seeds to a blender. Add garlic, salt and lemon juice. Blend until smooth.

4 Pour in the agar agar gel and blend for 20 seconds to mix.

5 Place in the freezer for 30 minutes to set. Store in the refrigerator after this.

BASIL RICOTTA CHEESE

This is a lovely savoury version of ricotta that is great for dipping.

MAKES 1 CUP

1 cup slivered almonds or 1½ cups blanched (without skin) almonds

1 tablespoon nutritional yeast flakes

2 tablespoons lemon juice (around 1 lemon)

½ teaspoon salt

½ cup water

¼ cup fresh basil leaves very finely sliced

1 Blend almonds in blender until fine and powdered.

2 Add remaining ingredients (except basil) and blend until smooth.

3 Place in a bowl and stir in the basil.

4 Refrigerate for 2 hours (or freeze for 30 minutes) to firm up.

TIP If you can only find almonds with their skin on, you can remove the skins by soaking in boiling water for 5 minutes, draining and squeezing off the skins.

LOADED VEGAN
CHEESE BOARD

A great entertaining combination.

MAKES 1 BOARD

16 oat crackers

12 wholemeal rice crackers

1 block vegan gouda cheese
(page 142)

1 block herby cashew cheese
(page 132)

beetroot hummus

pistachio nuts

cashew nuts

red and green grapes

strawberries

dried figs

dried apricots

olives

garnish: fresh Italian parsley

1 Choose a nice wooden board with a diameter of around 25cm (10in).

2 Arrange larger items first (e.g. cheese and crackers and bowls). Then fill in the gaps with the rest of the smaller ingredients.

3 To make beetroot hummus, simply add ½ cup of cubed and peeled raw beetroot to the classic hummus recipe (page 125) prior to blending.

TIP The cheese board will look best when all ingredients are clumped tightly together.

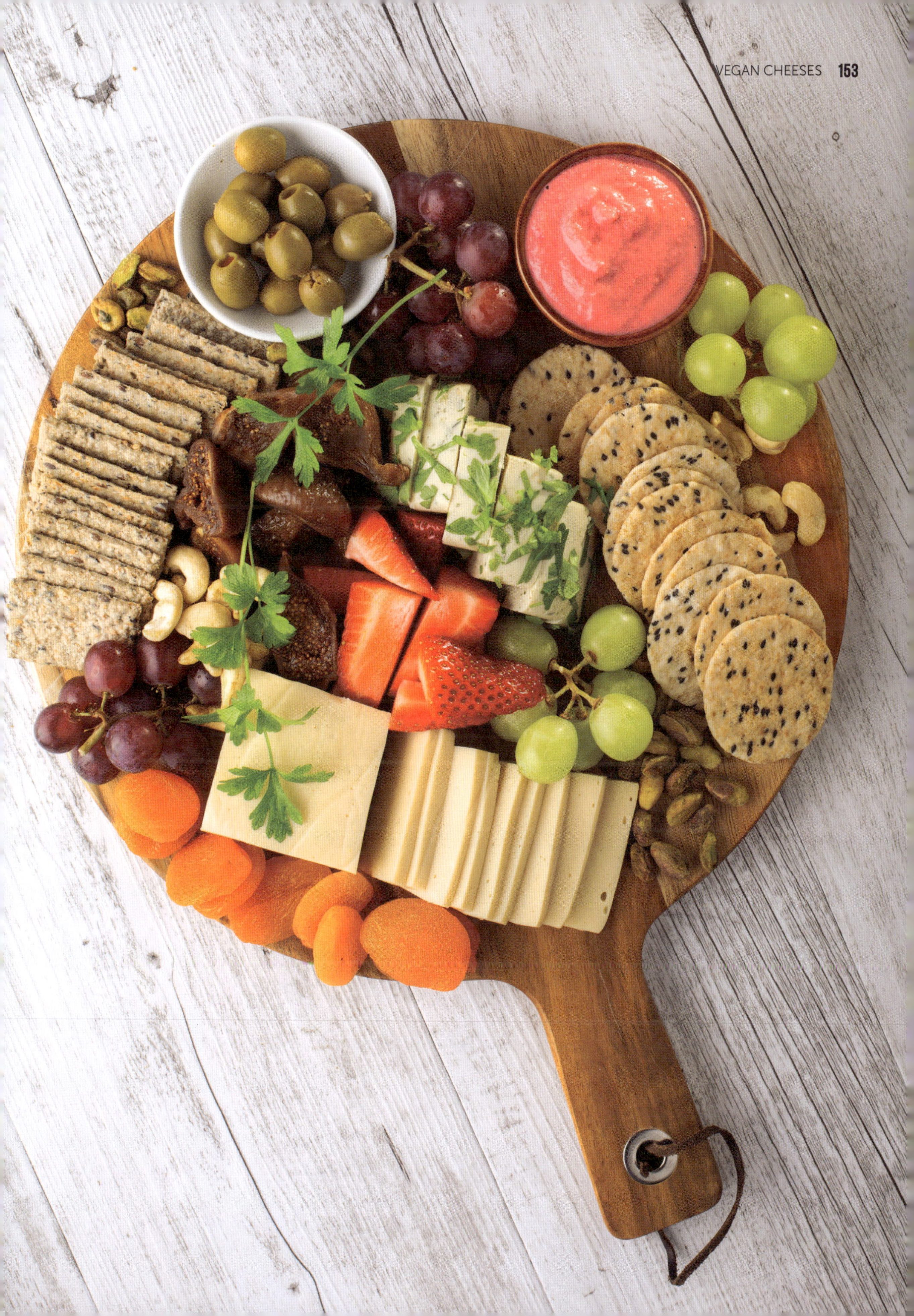

SWEET TREATS

TASTES TOO GOOD TO BE TRUE
TIRAMISU

This is an amazingly decadent plant-based version of the incredibly unhealthy dessert. This was the top seller in my cafes in 2018!

MAKES 9 LARGE SLICES

NUT BASE (BOTTOM)

1 cup almonds

½ cup dates

2 tablespoons caffeine-free coffee substitute powder (e.g. Caro, Inka, Ecco, Aromalt)

2 tablespoons coconut oil (melted)

2 tablespoons water

1 teaspoon vanilla essence

⅛ teaspoon Himalayan salt

MOUSSE (MIDDLE)

¾ cup almonds

¾ cup cashew nuts

½ cup dates

½ cup maple syrup

¼ cup almond milk

¼ cup coconut oil (melted)

3 tablespoons caffeine-free coffee substitute powder (e.g. Caro, Inka, Ecco, Aromalt)

CASHEW CREAM (TOP)

¾ cup cashew nuts

3 tablespoon almond milk

2 tablespoons coconut oil (melted)

2 tablespoon maple syrup

1 teaspoon vanilla essence

CACAO DRIZZLE (OPTIONAL)

1 teaspoon cacao or carob powder

1 teaspoon water

1 For the nut base, place almonds in a food processor and process into chunky pieces. Add dates and coffee substitute to almonds and process to a crumb. Add remaining nut base ingredients and process to mix.

2 Place baking (parchment) paper in 20cm x 20cm (8 in x 8in) dish and spread base mix with a spatula.

3 For the mousse, add almonds and cashew nuts to a blender and process until powder. Add dates to blender and process well. Add remaining mousse ingredients and blend until smooth.

4 Pour the mousse over the nut base.

5 To make the cream, place cashew nuts in blender and blend until powder. Add remaining cashew cream ingredients and blend until smooth. Spread over the mousse.

6 Place in freezer for 1 hour to set. Store in the refrigerator after this time.

7 Cut into squares to serve.

8 In a small bowl mix cacao or carob powder and water to form a thick pourable sauce. You will have to adjust to get the right consistency. Note that carob is a much darker colour than cacao.

9 Dust with extra cacao powder and pour over the drizzle to make it look amazing.

CREAMY MANGO &
PEACH PARFAIT
WITH PASSIONFRUIT COULIS

A lovely refreshing dessert. These 3 yellow fruits, peaches, mango and passionfruit, go together really really well!

MAKES 4 X 1 CUP SERVES

400g (12oz) can peaches drained (around 1½ cups)

1 cup mango chunks (if using frozen defrost in hot water)

garnish: mint leaves

PASSIONFRUIT COULIS

½ cup passionfruit pulp (available frozen in cubes)

1 teaspoon arrowroot

4 teaspoons cold water

1 tablespoon maple syrup

VANILLA CREAM

300g (10oz) firm tofu

6 tablespoons maple syrup

1 teaspoon vanilla essence

¼ cup coconut cream

1 Place cream ingredients into a blender and blend until silky smooth.

2 To make the coulis: Heat the passionfruit pulp in a hot pan. In a cup mix the arrowroot and cold water and then add to the pan. Add the maple syrup. Stir until it becomes thick. You may need to stir in a little more water if the texture is too gluggly and not pourable.

3 Layer for each glass as follows:
Top: a mint leaf
        ¼ of the passionfruit coulis
        2 tablespoons vanilla cream
        ¼ of the peaches
        2 tablespoons vanilla cream
        ¼ of the mango
Bottom: 2 tablespoons cream

TIP You can use frozen, pulp or fresh passionfruit. You can use frozen, fresh or canned mango.

DELECTABLE
RAW MOCHA SLICE

Yes that is a neat pattern of my front teeth in that photo and I immensely enjoyed eating this slice as you will too.

MAKES 18 PIECES

BASE

2 cups cashews nuts

1 cup dates

4 teaspoons coconut oil (melted)

1½ tablespoons smooth peanut butter

¼ teaspoon salt

MOCHA ICING

6 tablespoons coconut oil (melted)

1½ tablespoons maple syrup

6 tablespoons cacao powder

1½ tablespoons caffeine-free coffee substitute powder (e.g. Caro, Inka, Ecco, Aromalt)

1 Put base ingredients into a blender and blend until clumps together.

2 Place baking (parchment) paper in a 20cm x 20cm (8 in x 8in) baking tray.

3 Spoon the base into the baking tray and press down firmly with a spatula.

4 In a bowl mix together the mocha icing ingredients. Pour over the base.

5 Put the tray in the freezer for 1 hour to set. After this store in the refrigerator.

6 Cut into 3cm (1in) squares and serve.

TIP If your baking tray is too big just arrange the mixture at one end of the tray to achieve a depth similar to the photo.

VELVETY
VANILLA MOUSSE
WITH RASPBERRIES & PISTACHIO NUTS

This is one of those recipes that is embarrassingly simple to make. Just five ingredients into a blender and serve. Add a couple of attractive garnishes and wow! You will not believe how silky and velvety smooth this mousse is. Just ignore that there is tofu in this recipe or at least do not tell anyone!

MAKES 5 X ½ CUP SERVES

300g (10oz) silken tofu

4 tablespoons maple syrup

½ cup coconut cream

2 teaspoons vanilla essence

2 tablespoons lime juice (around 2 limes)

garnish: raspberries

garnish: pistachio nuts roughly chopped

1 Put all ingredients into a blender and blend for 30 seconds or until silky smooth.

2 Taste to test the flavour. You may need to add more maple syrup and/or vanilla to get a good flavour balance that is not too sweet and masks the tofu taste.

3 Pour into serving dishes and garnish with raspberries and pistachio nuts.

TIP If raspberries are not in season you can use frozen or any other berry.

PARTY IN YOUR MOUTH

PISTACHIO & ROSE
CACAO SLICE

MAKES 15 SLICES

The rose water and pistachio nuts take this chocolaty slice to an amazingly delicious level!

NUT BASE

½ cup almonds

½ cup cashew nuts

½ cup dates

2 tablespoons cacao powder

2 tablespoons coconut oil (melted)

CACAO CHOCOLATE

3 tablespoons maple syrup

½ cup coconut oil (melted)

3 tablespoons cacao powder

½ teaspoons cinnamon powder

¼ teaspoon salt

1 tablespoon rose water

TOPPING

4 tablespoons pistachio nuts roughly chopped

4 tablespoons dried cranberries

3 tablespoons goji berries

1 tablespoon cacao nibs

1 For the nut base, place almonds and cashew nuts in a food processor and process until chunky pieces. Add dates and cacao and process to a crumb. Add coconut oil and process to mix.

2 Place baking (parchment) paper on a 20cm x 30cm (8in x 12in) baking tray. Spread the base and press down firmly.

3 For the cacao chocolate layer, add maple syrup, coconut oil and cacao powder to a bowl and mix well. Add cinnamon, salt and rosewater and mix until well combined. Pour over the nut base and spread out evenly with a spatula.

4 For the topping, sprinkle pistachio nuts, cranberries, goji berries and cacao nibs evenly over the top. Press into the chocolate layer.

5 Place in freezer for 1 hour to set. After this store in the refrigerator for up to 2 weeks. Will soften when kept at room temperature, so eat quickly.

TIP Rose water can be hard to find. It is usually available at whole food or specialty stores. Some may have different strengths so you may have to adjust the quantity.

BITTER SWEET CACAO BALLS

These are a decadent form of Frooze Balls and a great chocolate substitute. They will need to be kept in the refrigerator as they have a high moisture content.

MAKES 24 BALLS

¼ cup coconut (fine or shredded)

1 cup dates

½ cup sultanas

1 tablespoon cacao nibs

6 tablespoons cacao powder

½ cup almonds

½ cup Brazil nuts

⅛ teaspoon Himalayan salt

up to 6 tablespoons of water

for coating: 2 tablespoons cacao powder

1 Put all ingredients into a food processor (except water and cacao for coating). Blend until fine. The mixture will clump up when it is getting close to being ready.

2 Slowly add a teaspoon of water at a time until the mixture is sticky but still holds together.

3 Put the cacao powder into a shallow bowl or plate.

4 Using your hands, roll into balls (around 1 tablespoon per ball) and place into the cacao bowl.

5 Coat all the balls in the cacao powder.

TIP Wet you hands with water before rolling the balls to minimise stickiness.

INCREDIBLE
CHIA BLUEBERRY
JAM

This is a lovely natural jam that has an amazing flavour and texture. It uses chia seeds as the healthy thickening agent. If you do not like chia seeds then you can grind or blend them first and use as a powder.

MAKES 2 CUPS

500g (16oz) frozen blueberries (around 4 cups)

4 tablespoons chia seeds

4 tablespoons maple syrup

1 tablespoon lemon juice

1 In a pot cook the blueberries for 5 minutes or until they are soft.

2 Add the remaining ingredients and cook for 5 minutes or until the chia seeds start to swell.

3 Stand for 10 minutes and transfer to a storage container. Will keep in the refrigerator for around 1 week.

TIP This jam is great served on wholemeal bread with sweet almond ricotta (page 149)

BLUEBERRY & BUCKWHEAT
BANANA PANCAKES

MAKES 12 PANCAKES

....

1 cup buckwheat flour

3 tablespoons
coconut flour

¼ teaspoon salt

1 teaspoon
coriander powder

1 cup rice milk (or plant-
based milk of your choice)

¾ cup water

2 ripe bananas mashed

3 tablespoons maple syrup

oil for frying 1½ cups
blueberries (fresh or
frozen)

garnish: chopped banana

garnish: extra berries (fresh
or frozen)

garnish: maple syrup

The perfect buckwheat pancake recipe according
to my wife Verity. These use banana to sweeten
and help hold them together.

....

1 Place buckwheat flour, coconut flour, salt and
coriander powder into a mixing bowl and mix.

2 Add milk, water, banana and maple syrup and stir until
evenly mixed.

3 Heat a non-stick frying pan and add a little oil.

4 Spoon ¼ cup quantities into the pan. Sprinkle around 6
blueberries onto the top of each pancake.

5 Cook for 2-3 minutes or until golden brown. Flip and
cook for another 3 minutes.

6 Serve garnished with chopped banana, berries and a
drizzle of maple syrup.

TIP You can use frozen blueberries, however make
sure you defrost them in some hot water first.
Frozen berries may prevent the pancakes
from cooking evenly.

BERRY & YOGHURT
AMBROSIA
WITH CARAMELISED NUTS & JELLY

MAKES 4 X 1 CUP SERVES

This is a lovely dessert with four different textures to get your taste buds very excited.

JELLY

2 cups boiling water

3 berry herbal tea bags

1½ teaspoons agar agar powder

3 tablespoons coconut sugar

CARAMELISED NUTS

¼ cup almonds

¼ cup cashew nuts

1 tablespoon maple syrup

MAPLE YOGHURT

1 ripe banana

300g (10oz) firm tofu

4 tablespoons maple syrup

½ cup coconut cream

1 teaspoon vanilla essence

FRESH BERRIES

1 cup blueberries

1 cup strawberries quartered

1 To make the jelly: Place water and herbal tea bags into a pot and bring to boil. Remove tea bags. Slowly add the agar agar powder, stir continually and cook for 1 minute or until dissolved.

2 Add the coconut sugar and cook for a further minute or until dissolved.

3 Pour into a 20cm x 20cm (8in x 8in) tray lined with baking (parchment) paper. Freeze for 15 minutes.

4 Place the slab of jelly slab on a board, remove the baking paper and slice diagonally to create random chunks.

5 To caramelise the nuts: In a pan heat the almonds, cashew nuts and maple syrup for 4 minutes or until very sticky. Stir as needed. Put pan into freezer (on a towel) to cool down for around 5 minutes.

6 To make the yoghurt: Place all the yoghurt ingredients in a blender and blend until smooth.

7 Place the berries, jelly and yoghurt into a serving bowl and partially mix. Garnish with the caramelised nuts. Serve immediately.

BREEZY SUMMER
GINGER & LEMON
SLICE

You need to try this lovely zingy citrus slice. It will melt in your mouth!

MAKES 12 SLICES

1 cup boiling water (to soak)

NUT BASE

½ cup dates

1 cup almonds

1 tablespoon ginger powder

3 tablespoon coconut
oil (melted)

LEMON TOPPING

3 tablespoons ground flaxseed
(linseed) (purchase ground or
grind with coffee grinder)

¾ cup lemon juice (around 6
lemons)

2 cups cashew nuts

½ cup dates

¼ cup maple syrup

¼ cup coconut oil (melted)

2 tablespoons lemon zest

¼ teaspoon turmeric powder

1 Put 1 cup of dates in boiling water to soak and soften for 10 minutes. Drain. Half is for the base and half is for the topping.

2 For the nut base, place almonds in food processor and process until chunky pieces. Add ½ cup soaked dates and ginger powder then process until it is a crumbly mix. Add coconut oil and process to mix.

3 Place baking (parchment) paper in 20cm x 20cm (8in x 8in) dish. Using a spatula spread the base evenly on the dish and press down firmly.

4 For the lemon topping, mix the ground linseed and lemon juice in a bowl and let it sit for 15 minutes or until it becomes a gel.

5 Add cashew nuts to blender and process until powder. Add ½ cup soaked dates and process well. Add the flax gel, maple syrup, coconut oil, lemon zest and turmeric and blend until smooth. Pour over the nut base.

6 Place in the freezer for 30 minutes to set. After this keep in the refrigerator. Slice into squares to serve.

DANGEROUS
CACAO MOUSSE
WITH PISTACHIO NUTS

This is so silky smooth and moorishly delicious that your family and friends
will not even realise it does not contain dairy, sugar or chocolate!

MAKES 4 X ½ CUP SERVES

300g (6oz) firm tofu (around 1 block)

¼ cup maple syrup

¼ cup coconut cream

¼ cup cacao powder

1 teaspoon vanilla essence

garnish: 1 tablespoon pistachio nuts

garnish: 1 tablespoon cacao nibs

1 Put tofu, maple syrup, coconut cream, cacao and vanilla essence into a blender and blend until smooth and creamy.

2 Place in the freezer for 20 minutes to set (but no longer as it will freeze). Then store in the refrigerator.

3 To serve, spoon into glasses. Garnish with chopped pistachio nuts and cacao nibs.

STRAWBERRY &
RHUBARB CRUMBLE
SLABS

I think rhubarb has a lovely flavour and when combined with strawberry makes these slabs of deliciousness!

MAKES 15 SLABS

2¼ cups rolled oats

1½ cups wholemeal spelt flour

¼ teaspoon Himalayan salt

6 tablespoons maple syrup

¾ cup coconut oil (melted)

2 cups rhubarb finely sliced (can use frozen or fresh)

2 cups strawberries finely sliced (can use frozen or fresh)

1 tablespoon lime juice (around 1 lime)

2 tablespoons maple syrup

optional: serve with sweet almond ricotta (page 149)

1 Place oats, spelt flour and salt into a mixing bowl and mix.

2 In another bowl mix the maple syrup and coconut oil together. Add to the dry ingredients and mix together well.

3 Select a baking tray 30cm x 20cm (12 in x 8in) and line with baking (parchment) paper.

4 Press ¾ of the mix into the baking tray. Keep aside ¼ of mix for the topping.

5 Place rhubarb, strawberries, lime juice and maple syrup into a bowl and mix well. Place on top of the crumble.

6 Sprinkle the remaining oat mix on top and press down lightly.

7 Bake for 45 minutes at 180°C (350°F) or until the crumble is golden and fruit is cooked.

8 Cut into squares and keep in the refrigerator.

TIP Optional: serve warm with sweet almond ricotta.

ENERGISING
BLACK FOREST
SMOOTHIE BOWL WITH BEETROOT

This amazing combination of cacao, cherries and beetroot could also double as a "fruit soup". A great meal for a hot summer day.

MAKES 2 SMOOTHIE BOWLS

SMOOTHIE

2 bananas frozen

1 cup cherries frozen

2 tablespoons cacao powder

1 cup rice milk (or plant-based milk of your choice)

1 tablespoon honey or date puree

½ cup raw beetroot peeled and chopped (around
1 medium beetroot)

TOPPINGS (PER BOWL)

6 frozen cherries

2 chopped strawberries

1 tablespoon chopped walnuts

1 teaspoon coconut chips

½ teaspoon cacao powder

½ teaspoon cacao nibs

mint leaves

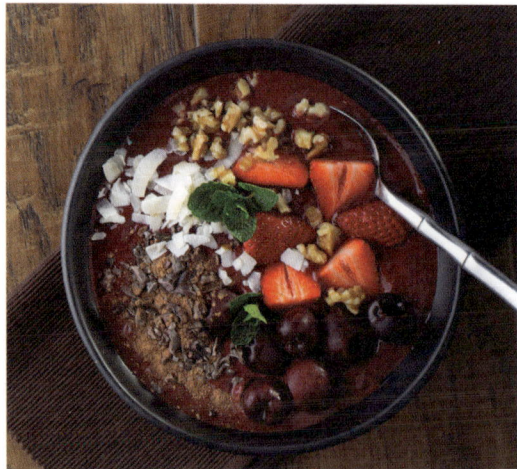

1 Place your serving bowls in the freezer for 10 minutes before serving to delay the melting process.

2 Put smoothie ingredients into a blender or food processor and process.

3 If your blender struggles or stalls, simply add more milk until it can blend freely.

4 Pour into bowls and sprinkle over toppings. Serve immediately as they will melt quickly.

REFRESHING TROPICAL
MANGO & KIWIFRUIT
SMOOTHIE BOWL

MAKES 2 SMOOTHIE BOWLS

This is a tropically inspired smoothie bowl bursting with flavour.

SMOOTHIE

2 cups frozen mango pieces

2 ripe bananas

1 cup rice milk (or plant-based milk of your choice)

TOPPINGS (PER BOWL)

1 kiwifruit peeled and cubed

½ cup frozen mango pieces (defrosted in hot water) or fresh mango pieces

1 tablespoons coconut chips

½ teaspoon black chia seeds

1 Place your serving bowls in the freezer for 10 minutes before serving to delay the melting process.

2 Put smoothie ingredients into a blender or food processor and process.

3 If your blender struggles or stalls, simply add more milk until it can blend freely.

4 Pour into bowls and sprinkle over toppings. Serve immediately as they will melt quickly.

BOYSENBERRY & CHIA
SMOOTHIE BOWL
WITH ALMOND BUTTER

A great way to have a smoothie. Use fruit in season or keep a supply of frozen fruit ready to go anytime. The almond butter is the star that makes this bowl combination awesome.

MAKES 2 SMOOTHIE BOWLS

SMOOTHIE

1 cup boysenberries

2 frozen bananas

1 cup rice milk (or plant-based milk of your choice)

TOPPINGS (PER BOWL)

1 tablespoon almond butter

2 tablespoons boysenberries (fresh or frozen)

2 tablespoons blueberries (fresh or frozen)

½ banana sliced

1 teaspoon chia seeds

2 tablespoons toasted muesli (granola)

1   Place your serving bowls in the freezer for 10 minutes before serving to delay the melting process.

2   Put smoothie ingredients into a blender or food processor and process.

3   If your blender struggles or stalls, simply add more milk until it can blend freely.

4   Pour into bowls and sprinkle over toppings. Serve immediately as they will melt quickly.

TIP Always keep some frozen banana in your freezer for smoothies. Take the skins off and rip into pieces before freezing.

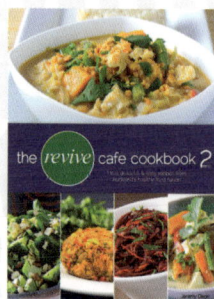

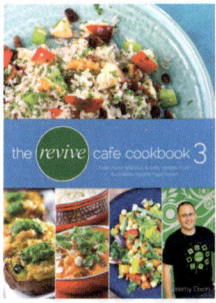

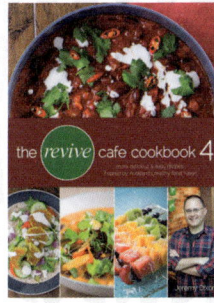

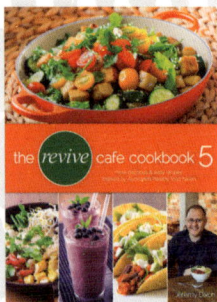

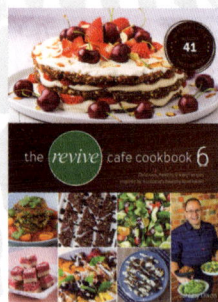

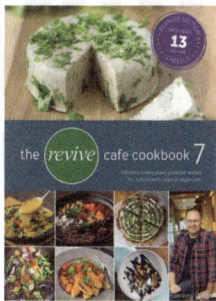